NIVE

The Creative College:
building a successful learning culture in the arts

The Creative College:
building a successful learning culture in the arts

edited by Graham Jeffery

Trentham Books

Stoke on Trent, UK and Sterling, USA

Trentham Books Limited
Westview House   22883 Quicksilver Drive
734 London Road   Sterling
Oakhill   VA 20166-2012
Stoke on Trent   USA
Staffordshire
England ST4 5NP

First published 2005

British Library Cataloguing-in-Publication Data
A catalogue record for this book is available from the British Library

ISBN-13: 978-1-85856-342-8
ISBN-10: 1-85856-342-9

Supported by NESTA, the National Endowment for Science, Technology and the Arts, an organisation that invests in innovators and works to improve the climate for creativity in the UK. For more information visit www.nesta.org.uk.

Cover: Photograph by Pau Ros
east london dance – Dancing Houses: Dancing Steps – 2002
Part of London Open House

Designed and typeset by Trentham Print Design Ltd, Chester an printed in Great Britain by The Cromwell Press Ltd, Trowbridge.

Contents

Acknowledgements

The book comes out of a long and sustained conversation and dialogue. It would have been impossible without:

Sid Hughes, Annie Cornbleet, Triche Kehoe, John Oram, Clare Connor, Jennifer Sims and Jacqui Mace, who along with me, started the conversation...

And who were joined over the years by

Ed Bennett, Rachel Bradbear, Nick Broadbent, Anton Califano, Angela Diskin, Laura Davies, Mark Hunter, Jill Hutton, Saci Lloyd, Uly Lyons, Steven Murphy, Martin McCloud, Sonia Khan, Mark Pearson, Giacomo Picca, Kishan Pithia, Jackie Sands, Fabien Senlanne, Seb Sutton, Roy Thomas, Keith Upton, Marc Ward, Robert Wells, Louise West, Paul Wakeling, Jane Wheeler

And our visiting artists, in particular: Deb Astall, Ben Ayrton, Alan Baptiste, Adam Benjamin, Danny Braverman, Martin Brown, Nick Cattermole, Evroy Deer, Chris Devaney, Bill Drake, Jasmine Fitter, Sean Gregory, Jonathan Grieve, Paul Griffiths, Hilary Jeffery, Katina Kangaris, Wayne Macgregor, Jade Persis Maravala, Miranda Melville, Deb Mullins, Dominic Murcott, Mark Murphy, Rowan Oliver, Mary Pearce, Marcia Pook, DJ Pogo, Dawn Prentice, Carl Reid, Tony Reid, Jenny Sealey, Sparkii Ski, Andrew Siddall, Hamish Stuart, Saburo Teshigawara, Ty, Simon Wring

We are most grateful to staff in the administration and finance teams at NewVIc who supported the projects even as they pushed the boundaries of systems: David Ball, Susan Barrow, Lesley Elgood, Tracey Stevens

All our colleagues at NewVIc deserve thanks, but in particular

Michael Dowd, Satnam Gill, Rob Damon, Jill Hutton, Suzanne Keys, Barbara Merritt, John Middleton, Steven Patmore, Bob Robinson

Our partners at Stratford Circus: Kiki Gale, Pamela McCormick, Gary Horsman and Tony Coleman and all their staff

At LIFT: Tony Fegan, Julia Rowntree, Anna Ledgard

Gorm and Nathan Gallagher at Bullet Creative

At the University of East London: Phil Cohen, David Butler, Gavin Poynter, Warren Lakin, Carole Snee and Loraine Leeson

At NESTA: Chloe Harwood, Sarah Maher, Gareth Binns and Clare Lovett

In Chicago Lott Hill, Julie Simpson, Carmel Avegnon Sanders, Jim Macdonald, Paul Camic, Phyllis Johnson, Brian Shaw, Monica Haslip, Paul Teruel and Cynthia Weiss

In Barcelona Eulalia Bosch, Ramon Espelt, Jaume Cela, Uta Staiger

Helpful leads and intelligent support, often in our darkest hours, came from Peter Renshaw, Nikki Crane, Adrian Chappell, and Shirley Brice Heath

Hundreds of students and ex-students – it would be invidious to name any of you individually but you know who you are!

A special thanks to Anna Craft, who patiently and tirelessly waded through pages and pages of purple prose in order to get the book to this point

The infinite patience and exceptional forbearance of our families, spouses, partners, friends and hangers on; and most especially I send love to Jackie, Finn and Thea Sands who have lived with this project for much longer than they deserved to.

Notes on contributors

Rachel Fell was the research assistant for the Pathways into Creativity project. Before completing an MA in Youth Work and Anthropology at Goldsmiths College, University of London, she worked in social research.

Andrew Blake is Professor of Cultural Studies and Head of the School of Cultural Studies at King Alfred's College, Winchester.

Kelly Davidson teaches Dance at NewVIc, and leads the Community Dance Practitioner programme in partnership with East London Dance. She has worked on a wide range of education projects with professional dance artists.

Sid Hughes is Principal of NewVIc.

Graham Jeffery is arts development manager at NewVIc and is currently seconded to the University of East London as Senior Lecturer and Programme Leader for Performing Arts.

Jo Parkes teaches Dance at NewVIc and also works as a professional choreographer. She has made dance films that have been screened on Channel Four and in film festivals worldwide, as well as leading community dance projects in Europe, Africa and the USA.

Abbreviations

ACVE   Advanced Certificate of Vocational Education

AS Level Advanced Supplementary Level GCE

ASDAN   Award Scheme Development and Accreditation Network

A Level   Advanced Level GCE

BERA   British Educational Research Association

BTEC   Business and Technician Education Council

BFD   BTEC First Diploma

BND   BTEC National Diploma

CABE   Commission on Architecture and the Built Environment

CoVE   Centre of Vocational Excellence

DCMS   Department for Culture, Media and Sport

DETR   Department for Environment, Transport and the Regions

DfEE   Department for Education and Employment

DfES   Department for Education and Skills

EAZ   Education Action Zone

EMA   Education Maintenance Allowance

ERDF   European Regional Development Fund

ESF   European Social Fund

EU   European Union

FE   Further Education

FEFC   Further Education Funding Council

GCE   General Certificate of Education

GCSE   General Certificate of Secondary Education

GOL   Government Office for London

GNVQ   General National Vocational Qualification

HE	Higher Education
HEI	Higher Education Institution
HEFCE	Higher Education Funding Council for England
HMI	Her Majesty's Inspector
HND	Higher National Diploma
ICT	Information and Communication Technology
LBN	London Borough of Newham
LDA	London Development Agency
LDDC	London Docklands Development Corporation
LEA	Local Education Authority
LEAP	London Education Arts Partnership
LIFT	London International Festival of Theatre
LONSAS	London Schools Arts Service
LSA	Learning Support Assistant
LSC	Learning and Skills Council
MP	Member of Parliament
NFER	National Foundation for Educational Research
NIACE	National Institute for Adult and Continuing Education
NACCCE	National Advisory Committee on Creative and Cultural Education
NewVIc	Newham Sixth Form College
NESTA	National Endowment for Science, Technology and the Arts
OCAP	Office of Community Arts Partnerships
OECD	Organisation for Economic Co-operation and Development
Ofsted	Office for Standards in Education
QCA	Qualifications and Curriculum Authority
RESCEN	Centre for Research into Creation in the Performing Arts
SCAA	School Curriculum and Assessment Authority
SME	Small or Medium sized Enterprise
SRB	Single Regeneration Budget
UEL	University of East London
UNESCO	United Nations Educational, Scientific and Cultural Organisation

Foreword

Sid Hughes

NewVIc was established in 1992 as a purpose-built, inner-city sixth form college. Being new meant that we were able to fashion a curriculum from scratch. But this brought with it a responsibility to justify our decisions about programme choice and resource allocation. Why, for example, given the limits on accommodation, should we allocate significant space to creative arts when local demand for subjects like business studies and sciences might outweigh our physical capacity to deliver them? The answer to this may be obvious to many, and perhaps the question itself considered unnecessary. But in these target driven times it is a question someone was bound to ask and they did.

Interestingly, it has been in the creative arts more than in any other area of the curriculum that we have been able to explore new territory for planning and implementation. For example, when setting up this aspect of our programme, a close relationship between the academic and the professional was essential, if only to help us with the design specifications for our small theatre, TV and media studios. But this relationship with the external and its subsequent impact on internal decisions and arrangements continued and grew and became one of the most significant factors in all that has happened since in the creative arts at NewVIc. It has inspired, as well as provided some of the solutions to, a whole series of crucial questions that we have been considering over the past decade.

How, for example, do we ensure a balance between the value of the college experience of creative arts with the life and career opportunities for our students? How do we promote the arts curriculum to the widest possible audience and address the generally accepted notion that young people who are unsuccessful in other areas of the curriculum find a natural home in the arts? How, as a sixth form college, do we build back into the community and contribute to public access to the arts even before our students come to us at sixteen, and after they have left us? How can resources geared to pro-gramme delivery and outputs be accessed to create opportunities which don't fit neatly into such a funding model? Similarly, how do we open up opportunities for staff so they can effectively contribute their own pro-fessional expertise and then, over time, encourage them to expand their skills and knowledge, so they grow and develop as professionals in a rapidly changing environment? How do we give our students access to a world of resources beyond the classroom so that their experience and opportunities are expanded? And how do we ensure that access to the arts and to the arts curriculum is truly access for all?

Introduction:
making space for creativity

Graham Jeffery

This book is the product of an unusual process and unusual circumstances. A team of teachers at Newham Sixth Form College (NewVIc) in East London developed a set of arts education practices that unleashed creativity through working collaboratively, focusing on the needs of individual students, and a curriculum that made use of a complex web of intra-organisational resources. They were given time, space and money to explore, document and situate their work in a larger context, in the two year period between 2002 and 2004.

The work they examined, and the process they used to explore it, has challenged boundaries: boundaries between schools, further education, higher education and the cultural sector; between models of professional practice rooted in community arts processes, vocational and academic teaching, between action research and detached critical analysis, and between young people, communities and the cultural industries. Over a decade the work of the NewVIc performing arts team has grown from providing small-scale vocational programmes for students aged 16 to 19 to encompass higher education, community learning, business support for the creative industries and professional development programmes for teachers and artists. Its success has been dependent on the determination of teachers to challenge orthodoxies and boundaries, working alongside sympathetic partner arts organisations, supported by managers who were not entirely risk-averse. They were determined to sustain and grow working relationships within and beyond the boundaries of the college, despite a climate of rapid and uncertain change.

The Pathways into Creativity research project sought to capture the essential features of this approach to teaching and learning. Putting this research project together, we have became acutely aware that little in our practices is genuinely new; it's a combination of personalities, personal histories, resources and, in many ways, favourable circumstances. Our work has drawn on distinguished practitioners, philosophies and approaches. So our work is thus not unique: there are superb examples of creative collaboration between colleges, schools and cultural organisations all over the UK and beyond. At NewVIc we have been fortunate in our combination of talented and ambitious staff, broadly supportive and encouraging managers and a rich and dynamic urban context for our work. And our debts to the visionary and skilled artists and teachers with whom we have collaborated, and from whose ideas our work flows, cannot be overestimated.

The relationships we forged have helped us understand that learning should never stop for teachers, that above all it is mobility and interaction across perceived organisational and institutional boundaries that teachers and students need if the profound barriers to learning and progression are to be overcome. We have been fortunate to have communicated with and visited some inspirational sites of learning around the world. But it would be wrong to pretend that the style of working argued for in this book is easy, suitable for every context, or without problems. The young people, colleagues, and the communities with which we work have continually thrown up new ideas, challenges and opportunities; and the biggest barriers to sustained innovation have mostly come from the institutional and policy frameworks within which we operate. There are profound structural inhibitors of creativity and innovation within education systems.

In this book we unpack some key features of this work. We share the approaches to curriculum design, some antecedents to our thinking, and resources, links and connections. As well as texts and projects, we have also referred to websites, all of which were live at the time of going to press, but may have a shorter lifespan than the book. What we present is inevitably marked by omissions, oversights and the biases and preferences of individual team members. The book touches only briefly on debates which have divided educators for centuries, about what is called 'fine art' and what is called 'popular culture' and their contested place in the official and hidden curriculum in schools, questions of aesthetics and value judgement, the relationship between the written and the oral/aural, the historical and the contemporary, between mimesis – imitation and rule-following – and creation. We write from our own experience as practitioners seeking to find a way through these debates. We hope, however, that this book will be a springboard and toolkit for teachers, artists and creative professionals, and those who work with them, who want to make the idea of a more inclusive version of creativity in education and education for creativity, work better.

Creative partnership is under-theorised and poorly understood. We have not attempted to provide a coherent or new theory of creative partnership – but we have sketched out some questions for further research. We refer to institutions of learning – schools, colleges, universities and other sites where learning might take place. At times we are unfocussed and unclear about whether we are talking about design and management structures for formal or informal learning, community learning or institutional learning, teaching and curriculum design in schools, further education or higher education. These are precisely some of the boundaries that our work has set out to challenge. The focus of our expertise, such as it is, has been in upper secondary, performing arts and media education for 16 to 19 year-olds. In recent years we have increasingly ventured into adult and community education, business support and incubation, and higher education. These are often considered to be discrete sectors, situated in a myriad of different funding, administrative and institutional arrangements, which throw up separate and particular problems. One of the major challenges over the last ten years has been to make sense of the contrasting and frequently con-flictual policy and funding frameworks within which our learning pro-grammes have to operate.

We argue for a different kind of learning institution and a different kind of teacher: that makes connections through partnership and collaboration to build individual learning pathways for students, teachers and people from the wider community, and for a working climate in which opportunities are embraced. We hope the stories that we tell in this book will help people in other places to seize such opportunities, wherever they are.

The project team
Generous funding from the Learning Programme of NESTA, the UK's National Endowment for Science, Technology and the Arts, enabled the equivalent of one and a half full time members of staff in the arts and media team at NewVIc to be relieved of teaching duties for two and a half years, from 2002 and 2004. This time was allocated dynamically and flexibly; it was used to release some staff from teaching for sustained blocks of time, while others explored their practice and reflected on their work in one day and weekend events and seminars. Staff made visits to different parts of the UK,

the US, France, Germany, Finland, Holland, Spain, Ethiopia and Argentina to participate in conferences, observe and investigate practice, lead workshops and projects and discuss our approaches with friends, allies and sympathetic critics. The project was led by Graham Jeffery, who spent three days a week working on it over the entire period and who spent the rest of his time continuing to manage and develop the relationships between the college, the University of East London, and the Stratford Cultural Quarter. He worked closely with Sonia Khan, the Creative Industries Development Manager, charged with leading and developing several large arts and re-generation projects. Rachel Fell was appointed as the project's Research Assistant for two years and proved invaluable as participant-observer, interviewer, writer and administrator. Three of the teaching staff had key writing responsibilities alongside Graham: Kelly Davidson, Jo Parkes and Andy Cobb. Other staff were involved in developing learning resources, film and video materials and web content, and everyone in the 27-strong arts and media team has fed into the discussion and debate provoked by this work. Artists Jackie Sands, Jonny McEwen and Sparkii Ski were commissioned to work alongside members of the team in developing reflection and evaluation of the interrelationships between their artistic practice and their work as teachers. Professor Andrew Blake, Head of Cultural Studies at University College, Winchester was commissioned to evaluate the college's relationship with the Stratford Cultural Quarter, and this is the subject of Chapter 6.

In the course of the research, interviews, discussions, seminars and workshops have been undertaken with our students, and partner organisations, in particular Urban Development, Theatre Venture, East London Dance, London International Festival of Theatre and the Guildhall School of Music and Drama. Through the work with NESTA, we also began a dialogue with officials from Arts Council England, the Department for Culture, Media and Sport and the Department for Education and Skills.

The project would not have been completed without the generous, sensitive, and unfailingly subtle and skilful mentoring and support of Anna Craft, Director of the Open Creativity Centre at the Open University.

The research process
The key aims of the Pathways into Creativity project were as follows:

■ To make explicit the methodologies that underpin the creative practice of performing arts teachers at NewVIc, particularly through exploring the philosophy of the teacher-artist

- To demonstrate, qualitatively and quantitatively, the impact of our curriculum practice on students' and teachers' motivation, learning, professional development and achievement

- To document approaches to the arts curriculum that build in sustainability, progression and development for all the stakeholders: students, teachers, artists and the wider community

- To implement, explore and document, with our students as co-researchers, some case studies in project design for the performing arts curriculum that engage participants in creative risk-taking, through contact with new people, spaces and learning processes

- To offer a critical analysis of the concept of creative partnership as exemplified in a number of key case studies involving NewVIc. Allied to this, to make regional, national and international connections and comparisons in order to engage with questions of empowerment, engagement and progression for young artists and arts educators

These rather ambitious aims were achieved in a variety of ways and with varying degrees of comprehensiveness, through an exploratory and interactive process. This book is one of the outputs from the project, which have also included educational resources, a website (www.newvic-creative.org. uk) and a series of events, presentations and performances which took place between April and November 2004.

We documented and evaluated four case studies which reflected different aspects of our practice. Three of these are found in this book as Chapter 3 (the BTEC First Diploma in Performing Arts), Chapter 4 (the dance-documentary film *Home*) and Chapter 6 (a study of the relationships between the college and the Stratford Cultural Quarter). Papers relating to a fourth case study, the community theatre project *Hair Pieces*, are available to download from the project website. Around these case studies we undertook a good deal of comparative study, reading, discussion and reflection. A second major strand of the project involved making contact with and visiting sites of learning involved in developing similar work, in the UK and abroad. This has begun a process of dialogue, to which we hope this book will contribute. The third strand of the research took the form of a small-scale collaborative project, led by Jo Parkes, between NewVIc teachers and teachers at Brockhill Park School in Kent. It sought to explore questions about the transferability of some of our approaches to the very different context of a largely rural secondary 11 to 18 school.

The project is the result of a long series of overlapping dialogues: internal, within the college, between members of staff; local, between the college, its staff and young people, its communities and stakeholders; regional, into the cultural and creative sector in London and beyond; national and international, as we sought out connections and conversations with people asking similar questions. It has seeded new collaborations and enabled a broader dialogue about the risks, rhetorics, realities and responsibilities of teaching and learning through creative partnership.

Inevitably, the book paints a partial picture of the work of the college and its partners. We have focused on activities and programmes based in the arts and media team at NewVIc, work that is only one small part of what the college is about. Our partner organisations also have many successful and innovative programmes of work which have nothing to do with the college, but which contribute to the vibrancy and creativity of the networks of opportunity we are part of. Many people contribute to the success of the college – above all the young people, but also their parents, teachers, administrative and support staff and the wider network of our supporters and partners. Classroom based work, teaching courses and getting young people through examinations, although it is central to our work, is only part of the picture. An important lesson from our work is that teachers need to develop the skills be able to navigate between, and influence, complex sets of relationships, from the micro, interpersonal level to the macro-level, the policy and institutional landscape. They can only do this if they have, or make, time to think carefully about what they are doing.

> The college ought to be a creative organisation looking for creative solutions. Creative ways of teaching, creative ways of guiding kids, creative ways of using the building. (Sid Hughes, Principal, in interview, 2002)

1

Creativity discourses and the arts: young people and uncertain futures

Graham Jeffery

The publication in 1999 of the report of the National Advisory Committee on Creativity, Culture and Education, *All our Futures* ignited a host of overlapping debates about the place of creativity in education that have been smouldering for decades. Other publications that were well received by the teaching profession followed, such as Seltzer and Bentley (1999), Craft, Jeffrey and Leibling (2001), and Robinson (2001). All called, in different ways, for a radical reconceptualisation of educational practices in the light of new insights about how the mind works, how economy and society is developing, and the role of investigative and participatory learning processes in fostering young people's identity-formation and engagement.

There are a number of reasons why creativity is advanced as key to the future of education. Some are based upon economic arguments stemming from the need for a redefinition of mass education – the need to educate a flexible and multi-skilled workforce, who need most of all to learn how to learn, in a society evolving rapidly into a knowledge-based or informational economy (NACCCE, 1999; Claxton, 2000; Robinson, 2001). Other arguments emphasise the importance of creative approaches in developing transferable skills such as flexibility, teamwork, resilience, initiative, and problem-solving (Lucas and Greany, 2000). Other theorists have developed a 'systems' or 'processes' approach to creativity which, based on research in social psychology and cognition, explore the relationships in learning between people, society, culture and knowledge generation (see Dust, 1999; Csikszentmihalyi, 1998; Feldman, Gardner and Csikszentmihalyi, 1994). There are also functional – and somewhat decontextualised – models of creative thinking processes based on research in the neurosciences which have been widely adopted in business, and are coming to prominence in education as 'tools' for expanding learning processes (see, e.g. Buzan, 2002; Baillie, 2003).

Other arguments about creativity in education focus on the concept of multiple intelligences (Gardner, 1983, 1993, 2000), which insists upon the need for education to be more effectively tailored to individuals, to reflect a much broader view of what constitutes knowledge, understanding and intelligence. Howard Gardner's work calls for a re-examination of models of teaching and assessment, in light of the understanding that there are many ways of experiencing, interpreting and representing the world beyond the narrow linguistic and logical-mathematical intelligences which dominate teaching, learning and assessment in schools. Teachers of the visual and performing arts have long argued from experience that these broader modes of expression can foster engagement and commitment in young people who are disengaged from other forms of learning but find ways of developing autonomy and self-knowledge through participation in the arts.

Arts practices provide a means of encountering the world through direct physical experience, utilising visual, auditory, tactile and other sensory stimuli, as well as text and diagrams, to involve students in making artistic work[1]. The incorporation of cultural practices from the young person's lifeworld into the world of the school or college through modes of arts education which allow young people space to explore and work with their own identities, interests and cultural traditions, provides a means of recognition and identification which allows them to engage with learning at deeper levels (see Brice Heath and McLaughlin, 1993; Kearney, 2003).

The work of psychologist David Perkins (1995) also suggests that intelligence cannot be measured in fixed or isolated terms. He identifies three foundations of intelligent behaviour: neural intelligence (the brain's underlying neurological functions, which depend for effective functioning on social, cultural and interactive learning), experiential intelligence (based on direct, accumulated experience of thinking or acting in particular situations) and reflective intelligence (based on exercising self-management and self-reflection). He asserts that better use of these capacities can be *learned*. Psychologist Robert Sternberg (1988, 1997) posits a 'triarchic' theory of human intelligence: analytical ability, creative ability and practical ability. Both Perkins and Sternberg's work have serious implications for the dominant models of teaching and learning in schools and colleges. Recent research by Shirley Brice Heath and Shelby Wolf (2004) points to the critical importance of fostering 'intent participation' in developing points of engagement and contact for young people, through activities which require immersion, concentration and close observation. Other studies have advanced the case for creative approaches as a means of recapturing auto-nomy, empowering teacher and student alike through the *active construc-tion* and interrogation of knowledge in the micro-world of the school com-munity (see, for example Craft, Leibling and Jeffrey, 2001; Craft, 1996, 2000b; Jeffrey and Woods, 2003).

In this book we have left to one side the debate about whether a focus on learning styles should dominate our thinking about teaching and learning, as it is raging elsewhere, not least in developing an understanding of what 'personalised' learning might mean in practice (see Miliband, 2004; Adey *et al*, 1999; Coffield *et al*, 2004). Instead, we adopt a broader, socially focused, and perhaps less technocratic definition of creativity, inclusiveness and 'personalisation' which seeks to meet the needs of the individual learner as part of a social whole.

There is a tendency to justify creativity in terms of its instrumental value as, on the one hand, a mode of learner empowerment, or, on the other, a means of producing knowledge workers for the new economy. Neither justification really tackles the underlying questions which creativity dis-course raises: namely, where in formal education is knowledge produced and transmitted, what forms of knowledge count, and what would be the features of learning institutions for a creative society?

> While it is fairly easy to show the relevance of creative practices for en-gaging learners and generating a commitment to learning, it is less easy to convince politicians and policy-makers that creative teaching and learning, which might also involve questioning current perspectives and practices, is beneficial to society. (Craft and Jeffrey, 2001, p9)

It is easier to fall back on justifications for creativity as being about nurtur-ing the exceptionally able or 'gifted and talented' (see for example, Torrance, 2000), than embrace the broader *critical* orientation implied by creativity's emphasis on questioning, acting upon and reconstructing knowledge, rather than simply reproducing it. As Seltzer and Bentley (1999 p25, original italics), point out: 'The key challenge is to shift the focus away from what people should *know* and on to what they should be able *to do* with their knowledge'. Many advocates for more creative approaches to teaching and learning suggest that mainstream educational policy and practice over-emphasises the transmission and transfer of set bodies of knowledge through standardised instructional methods and standardised assessment tasks. These treat the learner as a consumer of information, not an active participant in the construction of meaning. Surely, inquiry and questioning are fundamental for effective teaching and learning. Gordon Wells suggests that inquiry is valuable not simply for reasons of technical competence but because of an *ethical* imperative for teachers: 'to be the leader of a community of inquiry, one must be an inquirer oneself'. He writes of the

> ...serious and widespread failure to distinguish between knowledge and knowing... Because the outcome of the activity of knowing – that is, building knowledge together to solve a problem or create a new artefact – is frequently a representation of what has come to be known by those involved, it is often convenient to speak as if the knowing was captured in the representational product. From this, it is a simple step to speak as if the knowing could be transferred to another person simply by giving them the 'knowledge object'...

> From such a perspective, the purpose of schooling is viewed primarily as that of ensuring that students acquire the 'basic knowledge and skills' that they will need for daily life and employment after school and, for the college bound, the knowledge of the various subject disciplines that provides a basis for tertiary education...

> In other words, acquiring knowledge is largely separated from the situations in which, through knowing in action, knowledge is constructed and used. Graduates at each level 'know' a lot, but they are often neither able nor disposed to bring what they have learned to bear in the effective and responsible solving of real problems. Knowledge is treated like a commodity, to be amassed and banked (Freire, 1970), and occasionally displayed for show or as credentials when competing for further opportunities for capital acquisition. When grades and test scores are what matter, it is difficult indeed to encourage a spirit of inquiry and a quest for genuine understanding. For both teachers and students, in this sort of knowledge economy, it is hard to find a persuasive answer when asked 'what's in it for me?'(2002, p206-207)

If creativity is a universal 'function of intelligence' (Robinson, 2001, p111), then it is common to all domains and fields. However, in spite of the explicit rejection of creativity as only applying arts education in the NACCCE report (1999, p27), as Mathilda Joubert points out (in Craft, Leibling and Jeffrey, 2001), there is a tendency in policy thinking to see education for creativity and arts education as synonymous. The creativity agenda has been used to argue for a reformulation of the hierarchy of subjects within the UK's National Curriculum, but the place of a more generalised creativity in the curriculum beyond the area of the arts is contested, not least because there is little consensus about what creativity in education means, and many different and sometimes contradictory justifications of its purpose (see Craft, in press).

These debates are important because the struggles over the form and content of the school curriculum provide a lens through which broader social and cultural attitudes and norms can be viewed[2]. In this book, we focus more narrowly on the role of interpersonal and intra-organisational creativity, and specifically the concept of creative partnership in arts education, because this is our specialist area of experience. Whilst we fully endorse the idea that education in general could do with a more creative orientation, our work here focuses on the application of creativity to a particular set of performing arts and media education contexts. We hope that others will be able to develop and extrapolate from our conclusions creative practices in, for example, science, technology or humanities teaching.

Recent work by Anna Craft has conceptualised 'little c creativity' (as opposed to the 'high' creativity of the genius or global innovator) as involving at its heart 'possibility thinking' which permits acting out, flexibility of thought, problem-solving and making imaginative daily choices. She argues that the development of this type of thinking is an essential survival skill to be developed for life in the 21st century (Craft, 2000). Some of this work could be compared to the pioneering and detailed studies of the tactics used in the small acts, the cultural practices of everyday life undertaken by Michel de Certeau *et al* (2002), for example, cooking, looking after the house, everyday journeys and routines, and de Certeau's assertion that

> it is impossible to dissociate the act of understanding the environment and the desire to change it. 'Culture' obtains one definition from it: we can state the meaning of a situation only as a function of an action undertaken in order to transform it. A social production is the condition of a cultural production. (1994, p113)

Craft and de Certeau arrive at their conclusions about everyday creativity via different routes. Craft examines creativity from the standpoint of philosophical, pedagogical and ethical discourses. De Certeau illuminates everyday creativity through close observation and analysis from the perspective of cultural studies. However, both approaches foreground the everyday, the particular and the vernacular in understanding how people make sense of their lives and find small but meaningful ways of retaining a sense of authenticity or autonomy.

Two core principles underpin the working definition of creativity for the purpose of this study:

■ We emphasise creativity as a *critical* and *social* process, founded in social relations. We do not define creativity as an isolated and individual 'act of genius' but as *rooted in interaction* – the notion of the *creative milieu*[3] is important here: the need for places where relationships can be formed, connections can be made, collaboration can occur and resources can be obtained

■ The task for teachers and the brokers of learning, then, is to develop a microclimate where creativity might flourish – what we describe in this book as *building a learning culture,* so that students and participants are enabled to access resources, exercise critical judgement, undertake experiments and construct novel ideas, collaborate to problem-solve and produce work that is *of value to them and to the wider communities in which they are located.*

The conditions for creativity

A simpler definition of creativity might be to understand it as agency: as the ability and capacity to act and work with materials in order to produce ideas or products that are original and innovative in their context. Jason Toynbee (2000), writing about how and where creativity occurs in practices of making popular music, draws on Pierre Bourdieu's theory of 'habitus' (the disposition of the subject, who owns a portfolio of 'capitals' – cultural, economic, social) and the subject's interaction with a number of 'fields' – cultural, economic, social. Practice and invention – cultural production – takes place at the intersection of habitus and field, and for Toynbee is composed of small acts bound by a 'space of possibilities' which consists of the inter-related conditions – social, technological, cultural – in which the act of creation is undertaken. Organisations and teachers that want to foster creativity need to recognise that creativity takes place as a result of problem-solving and conflict; it is generated by a desire to change things, find new solutions, and lies at the intersection of routine/characteristics (what might be described in Bourdieu's terms as 'habitus') and the socially and culturally structured fields within which individuals practise. The notion of challenging and pushing established boundaries is central to this, as is an understanding of how the social conditions for creativity and the available resources (what Toynbee describes as the 'space of possibilities') limit or enhance new solutions and inventions. Amabile (1997) examines this set of issues from the point of view of social psychology and organisational theory.

We understand creativity as being composed of small acts and undertaken in communities of practice, and believe that a learning institution needs to provide *contexts* in order for this creativity to take place. We emphasise modes of learning which allow young people to act as social and cultural agents in their own neighbourhoods. We pay attention not only to the official curriculum as embodied in regulation, prescription, and assessment bureaucracies, but also to the informal cultural practices young people bring to the college. Working with extended networks and even across generations (see, for example, the account of the *Home* project in Chapter 4), the college is able to adopt an *intermediary* position which, we suggest, creates greater investment by individuals in their learning. Given the fragile and contradictory motivations for being in post-compulsory education, particularly amongst students who have been failed by schooling, who at 16 have not acquired the cultural capital of qualifications that have any currency in the labour market, there is a major task to be faced by teachers seeking to foster engagement and motivation. In Chapter 3 Rachel Fell and Kelly Davidson explore the dynamics of teaching and learning for a group of students who face multiple disadvantage. In such a situation, a focus on interpersonal communication, building trust and willingness to collaborate within the group becomes the key task. Many students bring a powerful agenda of resistance, anger, and resentment based on their experience of school before entering the sixth form college. Jane Wheeler, a teacher of this group, observed:

> Creativity to me means to be free to explore ideas and express oneself in different ways; free from fear of judgement and fear of failure. Students often seem to come to us with more than their fair share of both. I think their creativity can only be released when they can begin to get past all the defensive strategies they have developed to survive 'judgement' and 'failure'. Arguably, many of these [defensive] strategies are extremely 'creative' in themselves. (Email correspondence, 2004)

This remark emphasises the double-edged nature of creativity discourse. Claims of creativity are not value-free. Creativity, as a process of ideas generation, is used for many purposes. Not all manifestations of student creativity are necessarily approved by learning institutions, which raises questions about the exercise of power in a learning context. In moving creativity to the centre of educational thinking, do we risk sanctioning only an approved or accredited version of creativity?

The position(s) of the college

As an institution of post-compulsory education, the college occupies an interesting position at the end point of compulsory schooling. It forms a bridge between school, higher education and employment. Teaching 16 to 19 year olds is about helping them make the transition into successful and empowered lives – into higher education, or directly into meaningful work. The further education framework gives more flexibility than is possible in a school context: there is no compulsory National Curriculum, we work with long blocks of time, students are on more concentrated programmes and subject-groupings, and we teach many large-scale vocational qualifications (typically in 12-15 hours contact time per week), with teams of teachers involved in their delivery. Although we work with nationally agreed qualifications and a considerable volume of external assessment, there is still much greater flexibility and choice for learners than in most UK secondary schools. Chapter 2 tells the story of the college, its curriculum and its context.

From cultural economy to creative economy

Official descriptions of the cultural economy, of which both education and the arts could be seen as a part, seem to have become absorbed into the notion of creative economy. Perhaps this is because 'creative' is seen as a more neutral and less politically loaded term; it at least implies a constructive, generally inclusive and vaguely futuristic approach. As a rough working model, which incorporates everyday creativity as well as formal income-generating creative industry, the creative economy might be broadly conceptualised as a series of linked concentric circles, with far fewer full-time participants at the centre than the periphery:

■ creative industries – full time and part-time professional employment and generators of paid products for market, together with associated informational professions: journalism, advertising, marketing, multimedia, ICTs. This is the sector of the creative economy most mapped (see O'Connor, 1999; DCMS, 1998, 2001). This core also includes publicly funded institutions providing cultural products and services – museums, galleries, theatres, venues etc.

■ participatory and learning-driven cultural activity – a source of employment and rapid growth for cultural providers – publicly and privately funded through a mixed economy with a whole raft of activities categorised as learning, participatory, audience development

▪ non-formal participation in cultural activity in everyday cultural life: unpaid participation in a myriad of everyday cultural practices – bedroom studios, voluntary activity, clubs, societies, religious activity, sport and leisure

Pointers to the scale and importance of the sector tend to be found in measures of corporate turnover, export figures, or numbers of employees, many of whom in the 'creative industries', in a corporate-capitalist context, are likely to be employed in mundane clerical or support operations familiar from any corporate environment, with nothing particularly creative about their occupational roles. But there are also the multitasking, multi-skilled cultural intermediaries in the world of the SMEs, micro-businesses and freelancers who service and feed the corporate-cultural-community food chain, and considerable numbers of participants in informal cultural activities, religious ceremonies or unpaid labour in bedroom studios (see Blake and Jeffery, 2001a, 2001b).

Unsurprisingly, most maps of the cultural economy exclude informal and voluntary participation and so-called pirate and underground economies of cultural production: for example graffiti, unlicensed radio, clubs and street fashion. Such forms of cultural expression have vital and direct relevance for young people in navigating their everyday lives and learning. There are many other recreational or religious forms of cultural consumption or expression. They provide some of the most crucial ties that bind together communities, add value and distinctiveness to neighbourhoods, and allow communities to represent their interests within the metropolis (see Finnegan, 1993; Willis, 1990, 1993; Wali *et al*, 2002). These forms of cultural proto-economy may also subvert established consumer-producer divisions and hierarchies and provide spaces in which interchange might most readily be activated.

An exclusive focus on the economic value of culture and its role in creating the 'symbolic capital' (Zukin, 1995) with which cities compete for the business of the 'creative class' (Florida, 2002) tends to ignore the significance of informal and unofficial participation in everyday cultural activity. Florida (2002) describes a world governed by markets, by the consumer and lifestyle choices of the creative class and by the dizzying and disorienting effects of flexible globalised capitalism. The highly educated, highly mobile and highly skilled creative class takes advantage of the opportunities for rapid relocation – and wealth accumulation – afforded by the knowledge economy. According to Florida's schemata, cities need to attract innovation by providing a milieu in which the creative class feel comfortable. Although his watchwords for a successful and creative city include 'diversity' and 'tolerance', he also acknowledges the polarising effects of this dynamic, as urban regions splinter and socio-economic inequalities multiply in the face of a hungry consumer society and rapid economic restructuring (see Graham and Marvin, 2001). But as Ann Daly points out, the mythologisation and depoliticisation of the social status of artists, as either 'happily starving' (Daly, 2004: p2) or as aspiring, uncritical businesspeople or entrepreneurs in Florida's vision of the creative class is controversial: 'Many cultural theorists like to see cultural forms such as graffiti art and rap as political movements expressing the voices of the oppressed. This absurd notion does a disservice to both politics and art' (Florida, 2002, p201).

There are serious risks associated with an uncritical and depoliticised celebration of creativity, or one in which economic value is the final arbiter of cultural value. Creativity is increasingly being used as 'the concept that acts as a mediator between art and culture, between industry and technology' (Sasaki, 2004). It is used to describe the process of invention and *making*.

Creativity and culture

Within creativity discourse, the three competing definitions of culture which dominate thinking about arts activity, culture as high quality art (or Art with a capital A or, perhaps, 'complex culture' as Jowell (2004) puts it neutrally but blandly), culture as economic activity (culture as industry – still associated more with popular culture than so-called high culture), and everyday culture, can fairly readily be elided into a generalised and unfocused creativity. Generalised definitions fail to acknowledge contextual and cultural difference and run the risk of downplaying conflict, struggle and the political and social positions of those undertaking the 'creative act.' From 1997, New Labour sought to include all forms of culture under the umbrella of the 'creative industries', thus in a single move appearing to equalise and democratise: opera to punk, ballet to bhangra. This discourse was driven in part by a version of cultural economics which defined all cultural formations as creative assets, which, through enlightened policy thinking might mobilise communities, educate populations and unify the nation in a drive towards a modernised future under the banner of 'excellence, innovation, regeneration and access' (Smith, 1998, p19). As the Culture Secretary wrote: 'Creativity, culture, national identity and the nation's future wealth are all inextricably bound up together. It is skilled, creative people that make the difference. And the proper role of the government is to *enable* that to happen.' (Smith, 1998, p147, original italics)

Cultural education, then, is caught between three contemporary discourses:

■ an economic discourse in which creativity and culture are central to the nation's position in the competitive global economy (see DCMS, 2001)

■ a social discourse which emphasises access, inclusion, participation and the social value of arts participation (see Matarasso, 1997)

■ aesthetic and craft discourses which form some of the historical foundations of arts education (see Eisner, 2004; Wakeford, 2004)

The arts and social value

The drive to increase access to and participation in the arts for all communities has brought issues of cultural diversity, education, access and inclusion into sharp focus. The arts community is vehemently divided over how to respond to a governmental agenda of access and inclusion (see Kester, 1999; Wallinger and Warnock, 2000). A long history of collaborative and socially engaged arts practices[4], alongside 'subcultural' and underground forms of popular cultural production, have been harnessed to a policy agenda pulled by the twin horses of social inclusion and creative industry. This creates ethical and practical dilemmas for practitioners who identify with radical traditions of community arts and community education, or who seek to challenge or criticise globalised models of business or industrial relations. As inclusion moves to the centre of policy rhetoric and creative partnership is now officially funded to the tune of millions of pounds per annum, questions of definition, purpose and ethics assume greater urgency.

There are many examples of socially engaged practice, often attaching arts-making processes to the objectives of learning, outreach or participation: between schools, colleges and universities, between professional, voluntary and community organisations, and between artist-practitioners and community participants. In Chapter 5, I explore how some of these strands of practice weave together in the formation of the notion of artist-educator or teacher-artist.

Many of these new hybrid arts-education-regeneration projects defy being placed into the simple categories of education or inclusion or access. They work across the boundaries of traditional descriptive or aesthetic categories. Such practices, particularly in the visual arts, have been described as 'littoral' – as lying 'on the shore' or in an 'in-between' or liminal space

(Kester, 1999). Practitioners engaged in such work find themselves caught between policy imperatives which require either an economic definition of the arts, or which define arts activities in terms of their social utility, as crime diversion, youth development or social inclusion, or which occasionally cling to elitist definitions of excellence; in which 'classical' arts practices are seen as somehow transcendent of markets, industries, politics or class interests. Another strand of arts education research, particularly prevalent in the US, seeks to test whether participation in arts based learning processes can have demonstrable and measurable effects upon young people's test achievement, and social and intellectual skills[5]. All these policy and evaluation approaches have pitfalls which have been discussed extensively elsewhere (see, eg. Blake and Jeffery, 2001a, 2001b).

People running arts projects which cross sectors and traditional boundaries frequently complain about problems of sustainability, with multiple, overlapping and sometimes contradictory funding regimes, and a constantly shifting policy focus, which make long term development difficult to embed[6]. Reliance on project funding means that continual re-invention and re-working is needed; in some ways this might spur entrepreneurship and innovation. To be genuinely transformative, models of inclusive practice need to be allowed to become developed, refined and embedded over time. In a climate of short-termism, sustaining partnership working becomes dependent on the commitment and energy of key individuals. Without long-term models of organisational development for partnership, which encourage leadership succession (the capacity to sustain and develop leadership beyond the single inspirational individual, upon which so many innovative projects rely), projects are left in a fragile state.

Moving beyond an enthusiast culture, in which innovation in the arts and learning is driven by committed and, some might say, unrealistic individuals, and into sustainable professional models of working in new ways, requires a serious commitment to achieve structural change – in the conditions of institutional relationships and the patterns of teachers' and artists' working lives. The arts sector is engaged in a parallel struggle to develop forms of leadership, engagement, capacity and capability for cross-sector partnership working. Challenges and responses to this agenda are explored further in Chapters 5, 6 and 7.

What *is* clear, however, is that, however the underlying motive is rationalised, such inter-agency and cross-sector working is becoming a central feature of the institutional landscape. Linked to the agenda to widen participation in higher education, promote lifelong learning, and develop the creative industries economically, partnership working between the arts sector and education institutions becomes a powerful tool. It is often claimed that creative partnership can make a difference to the aspirations of artists, teachers, cultural providers and learners.[7] There is also an increased focus on finding ways of developing sustainable and inclusive pathways into participation – and beyond participation, careers. Underneath such operational questions of widening participation in the arts, now beginning to be framed in the language of 'cultural entitlement', lies another, less frequently answered set of questions: widening participation into *what*, and *for whom, on whose terms*, and *for how long?*

An argument is emerging that to combat the exclusionary tendencies of creative clusters, different types of higher and further education are required. This might mean that courses would not solely be delivered in a single institution. They might take place *between* community and industry settings. Increasingly we are seeing education that is delivered collaboratively between a learning institution and its partners outside, or even entirely through models of workplace apprenticeship. By engaging learners in a wider variety of contexts, the argument goes, learners work in ways that are more relevant and situated, and are able to develop practical and professional skills in the workplace.

Underlying this is the notion of *dialogue* – that educators need to enter into conversations with individuals and groups whose needs they have not yet met adequately in order to learn from them, and also to develop a meaningful dialogue between educational providers and the communities they serve – employers, local people, public, private and voluntary sectors. Paulo Freire's notion of 'dialogical' rather than 'banking' education[1] is useful here (see Freire, 1970, 1998a, 1998b). But without a commitment to critical analysis of the social dynamics and power relations embedded in such dialogue between education institutions and the communities of interest that they serve, together with a strong framework for evaluating the pedagogical effectiveness of such partnerships (see Chapter 5; Muschamp, 2004; Ross, 2003), the notion of creative partnership may become a euphemism for inequitable and illusory relationships which have little long-term transformational potential for learners.

Inclusion and arts education

Inclusive artistic practices are first and foremost practices which are not exclusionary, restrictive or judgemental. This is problematic and paradoxical because cultural traditions and practices, or communities of practice depend for their definition on including and excluding some traditions, languages of performance and cultural forms. This is often why radical practitioners choose to challenge certain traditional modes of teaching, learning, and cultural production. The irony is that any tradition, to survive as a set of practices, depends on constant renewal and reinvention[8] – and that we all operate, whether we like to think about it or not, within multiple and overlapping sets of discourses, cultural practices, and language forms which are the basis of any communication[9].

In this book, and in our teaching, we prefer to think of artistic practices, for the sake of learning, as being governed by an inclusive definition of cultural activity and cultural economy – which incorporates informal everyday creativity as well as more formal cultural activity. By formal cultural activity I mean that which is income-generating, which is bought or sold, or bound up with 'high' cultural traditions and institutions. Essentially, we are arguing for a notion of *cultural democracy* – in which access to and participation in culture fully acknowledges cultural diversity, is open and not over-determined or over-written by so-called classical cultural forms, which is not to deny the importance and living significance of cultural legacies and traditional artforms, or to say that they are not to be studied or practised. It's also about the understanding that all cultural forms, no matter what they are, or where they come from, are socially constituted – that they arise out of particular sets of social, economic, and political conditions, histories and narratives, and need to be understood as such. Many of the models of arts learning that we explore in this book displace activity from the formal social context of the college and move it into other social locations where the arts are practised – the club, the theatre, the warehouse space, the street. This reflects the stance of the college as not seeking to become an authoritarian arbiter of cultural value. Instead it enters into dialogue with the communities it serves, to the point where it shares spaces and develops shared programmes of work with community partners (see Chapters 6 and 7). Tony Bennett (2000) explains cultural democracy like this:

> In complex, culturally diverse societies, there is no single hierarchy of cultural values in play of the kind that was supposed in the earlier development of western cultural policies. This is now widely recognised in official cultural policy discourse – e.g. the Council of Europe text *In from the Margins*, or UNESCO's *Our Creative Diversity* – as the shift from a culture and democracy perspective (striving to equalise conditions of access to an accepted standard of high culture) to one of cultural democracy (aiming for dispersed patterns of support based on an acceptance of a parity of esteem for the aesthetic values and tastes of different groups within culturally diverse societies). (2000, p4)

Working in an impoverished multiethnic context such as Newham constantly foregrounds the tensions between the canonic and post-imperial definitions of high culture which still haunt the official curriculum[9] and the dynamics of inclusion/exclusion, lived through the complex and multi-layered personal histories, and attitudes to and experiences of institutional practices, which define young peoples' identities in the contemporary global city (see Kearney, 2003). The NewVIc response to this has been to focus strongly on contemporary arts practices, particularly those generated by artistic practices drawn from popular, hybrid and diasporic cultures. But it brings a strong commitment to debating, analysing and revealing the multiple histories embedded in contemporary culture, and uses the making of *new work* as a way of revealing, exploring and learning from long-established repertoires. An inclusive definition is required of what counts as a cultural/ historical tradition in arts education. As qualifications content has also shifted to acknowledge a greater diversity of histories and traditions within art-forms, through partnership working we have also been able to draw upon live work and the testimony of professional artists working in many different traditions, from scratch DJs to orchestral musicians, from performance poets to Shakespearean actors. And of course many of these individuals continually work between and beyond so-called classical and popular genres in their professional lives.

Working with our own cultural histories and those of the officially sanctioned curriculum, we teachers impose plenty of our own cultural biases and norms, and there needs to be some space for dialogue and debate over the form, content and outcome of the learning processes within which students and teachers work. This is not an argument for cultural relativism but rather for critical interrogation and creative re-invention, through dialogue, of the different cultural inheritances that comprise the arts learning landscape. The young people themselves are ideally placed to activate this dialogue, as agents who negotiate between inheritance and innovation in their own forms of cultural expression, whether in popular musics or street dance, religious ceremony or family music-making, or in their learning within prescribed and formalised frameworks of arts qualification systems.

Because they understand these tensions, advocates of cultural democracy and inclusive practices insist that the local, the small and the particular are important. Instead of the entertainment business, mass cultural forms or even, in some instances, building-based work, community arts practitioners tend to focus on the role of art-making in the formation of individual identities, empowering individuals, and in raising and responding to social, political or ecological questions, global and local. Chapters 4 and 5 outline ways in which the NewVIc team tackled this agenda.

In a useful summary of the debate, Charles Landry and Marc Pachter (2001, p23) point out

> Today, these three strands of culture – the avant-garde, the popular and that concerned with social development – together with the continuing idea of the traditional culture of refinement, are in tumultuous interplay, causing a confusion of aims for those working in the cultural field. Traditional high culture advocates often feel under siege in the demand to justify their existence through a commitment to democratic objectives, which places on culture what they see as the extraneous burden of social or political goals. Avant-garde culture challenges and is challenged by majority standards, alternating between the stance of aloofness and the embrace of radical social visions. Those in the group who see culture's purpose primarily as the achievement of broader social aims such as community development and the encouragement of diversity and empowerment fight what they consider elite privilege and insular purpose in both traditional and avant-garde high cultures. And all, in different ways, confront an entertainment standard, with its emphasis on amusement or consumption as an arbiter of value.

An inclusive rationale for participation in cultural activity would draw on notions of everyday creativity (e.g. Craft, 2001), community and mental health and wellbeing (see White, 2004) aiming to develop the capacity to communicate, engaging with the textures of everyday life to involve people in cultural production rather than simply consumption or reproduction of what is produced by the market (see Willis, 1990; Matarasso, 1997; Sefton-Green, 1999).

Choreographer Adam Benjamin has written about the inclusive politics of participatory artistic processes. He proposes that the mechanism of inclusive leadership is essentially about problem-solving; a pedagogy that is open about questions, uncertainty and difficulty. In this extract from his excellent book *Making an Entrance*, he is writing about the design of dance programmes that are inclusive of disabled students, but these principles have much wider application:

> Each new student in our class should encourage us to re-evaluate the body and the body of knowledge that we have come to take for granted... Perhaps the most important issue for new courses to bear in mind is that integrated practice is about problem-solving, and that rather than trying to fit new students into pre-existing structures, the course itself should be geared to address and deal with problems as they arise, and should there-

fore be structured flexibly in order to do so. It is hoped that any new intake of students (on any course) will identify shortcomings with course content and delivery... It is an approach which demands that any theorising be linked with a commitment to effect change. Such an approach is clearly at odds with much of current dance teaching, which is more commonly about following instructions rather than asking questions. (Benjamin, 2002, p8-10)

The processes of developing participation in the arts can thus be conceptualised as a problem-solving praxis, in which the leader and participant are encouraged to maintain an openness about outcomes and a dialogue about problems that arise in the course of the learning. This is theorised best in the work of Paulo Freire. It makes use of a social model of the construction of difference (see Benjamin, 2002; Shakespeare, 2000), in which, understood in relation to disability,

> ...a person is disabled by the way that society is organised, not by his/her own body, Disabled students are not dis-abled by their bodies or wheelchairs, but by the fact that the dance studio is up a flight of steps or a teacher teaches a class based mainly on footwork without reference to them. A blind student is disabled by a teacher who only demonstrates visually... (Parkes and Connor, 2004, p8)

This social model of disability has been further refined by, amongst others, John Swain and Sally French (2003), who propose an 'affirmative model' of disability based on the experiences of the disability arts movement, which seeks to establish 'non-tragic' representations of the experiences of disabled people, rendering difference visible and asserting identities positively (see Kuppers, 2003). Beyond a shallow rhetoric of 'celebrating difference' – which could be regarded as a recuperative strategy anyway – a more inclusive learning culture needs to be constructed 'in which we are visible, affirmed and valued, [and which] is also one in which we are more able to actively participate and to take the risks involved with being a learner' (Nind *et al*, 2003, p164).

So an inclusive process has two sides. One is questioning taken-for-granted or socially conditioned notions of what constitutes 'quality' and 'excellence', challenging assumptions about the motivations for cultural participation. The other is an intense focus on the needs of the participants and an openness to dialogue and debate about what they want – simultaneously providing an appropriately affirmative, demanding and challenging framework for participation. In one sense, accessibility is more about the style of delivery than it is about the content of delivery because technology and adaptation of technique allows accessibility – provided that there is always an openness about what is permissible as a technique, adapted to what individuals can actually do.

> Integrated groups involve bringing together people who have been separated on the grounds of untruths, i.e. on the basis of superstition, ignorance and economics. So in an integrated dance group, you have to be able to develop antennae capable of spotting reoccurrences or outbreaks of charity or superstition when more apt or enlightened means of communicating or behaving can be found. To quote Nicholas Malebranche, we should seek justice before dispensing charity.
>
> That may not always be easy, it may mean questioning a value judgement that you have grown up with, and that everyone around you regards as normality, But you have to be able to spot it (that's the ethics part) and if you are to succeed, to make it visible, by humour, by exaggeration... by devising alternative strategies, by any means possible through your art (that's the aesthetics part). (Benjamin, 1999, p2)

Graeme Evans and Jo Foord make some interesting observations about the dynamics of inclusion and exclusion:

> It is therefore important to theorise and operationalise empirically – from what are individuals and groups being excluded and on what basis? An individual can only be regarded as being excluded from activities if they would like to participate... Clearly in a diverse society the relationship between social exclusion, social integration and public choice is a complex one. In this respect we perhaps need to research the new models of inclusion (which paradoxically may be individual and privatised), as a recent European Union study concluded, 'because social inclusion coexists with (or in fact be caused by) inclusion, research on exclusion cannot be disconnected form the analysis of change on the 'included' side of society' (European Union, 1998). (2004, p181)

At NewVIc we have always argued that inclusion has to start with change on the side of the institutions and individuals seeking to include. That is to say, there is a social and ethical responsibility upon cultural institutions – and any other institution, funders and governments and businesses, for that matter – to adapt and challenge their own assumptions and hidden prejudices in order to include the communities that they serve.

Sid Hughes, the principal of NewVIc, explains in his own words how the notion of inclusion began in the context of the college:

> A student isn't something that is uniform; a student is a living being. Some of them are wonderful creatures, and some of them are a pain in the backside. You have to work with whatever comes your way. And work with them

towards educational goals and life experience goals. Now there are several ways of achieving what you want with young people: you can either say okay, we want so many people to pass their exams, and what we do therefore is select the ones that are most likely to pass their exams and teach them, or you can take the view we take, [which] is, if we feel a young person has the potential for work at a particular level, let's [take them], even though they may have minimum qualifications.

We will work with them and do all that we possibly can to make sure they're successful. We won't put hurdles in their way... Now I know barriers are often referred to; we talk about the college being barrier free in terms of disability so that we reduce the number of barriers for young people who are seen with mobility problems in getting around the place. But a barrier free institution is more than that; it's actually getting rid of the barriers to participation.

Q *What kind of barriers?*

The first and fundamental barrier is just whether or not a person can get into your college. How are you judging them: you look at their past record, you look at their behaviour, their GCSE results and if you simply look at GCSE results and say to a young person 'we'll only take you if you've got these particular results', then that's the first barrier [they face] if they haven't got them. What if those coming without GCSEs, you decide you're not going to take them, they're less worthy than those who have got good GCSE results already. And we took that decision not to do that.

That was in some cases the most difficult decision for our first staff meeting. I remember this vividly, because of having explained this notion as being at the centre of our organisation. The first challenge to that came from some members of staff who wanted me to raise the entry requirements for the kids applying to the college. So here we had all this explanation going on about the college being barrier free, open access, and also the staff were appointed on that basis, and I have a meeting of our staff who then say: 'Sid, we really ought to raise the entry requirements' which was completely opposite to what we had agreed up to that point. Which was a bit of a nightmare. I was quite shocked. I thought, my God, I thought we'd all agreed this. And here they were saying, if we do this we know it won't work. And I said no, no it won't work if you don't teach them properly.

So we had to go back to not blaming students. In those days, when things didn't go well, teachers in schools and colleges everywhere blamed the students, said they're not up to it, and we turned that round and said, no actually if we're taking these students into our college and they don't achieve, what we've done is not appropriate, we haven't taught them properly. We can't take the credit for teaching kids and be successful on the one hand if we're not prepared to say [on the other, that] when they haven't been successful we haven't taught them properly. Now that's a fundamental shift and that's the difference... between us and many other institutions. Many other institutions still blame kids for poor results... Right? And we don't. And we won't have it.

In Chapter 2 and the following case studies we explore how this agenda played out in the interactions between the NewVIc performing arts team, its partners and the wider circle of surrounding communities. It could be argued that some of our approaches represent a form of personalised learning, although this phrase was not in our vocabulary when we began this study. We would prefer to think of our approach as representing person-centred learning, which has as its basis the understanding that all individuals are unique and bring their own experiences, questions, values and assumptions to the learning setting. As educators we too are on a learning journey; the cultural and artistic assets of the cities and communities in which we live and work, produce and provide a rich set of resources for learning and development for the whole college community.

Notes

1   For recent research in this area see McNorton (2002) on drawing 'physically'. See also Benjamin (2002) and Kuppers (2003). Tufnel and Crickmay (1993) has also become a central text in our teaching of physical improvisation and devising for performance.

2   Swartz (1997 p189), on Pierre Bourdieu's sociology of education: 'Bourdieu sees the educational system as the principal institution controlling the allocation of status and privilege in contemporary societies. Schools offer the primary institutional setting for the production, transmission and accumulation of the various forms of cultural capital. More importantly for Bourdieu, schools inculcate the dominant systems of classification through which symbolic power is expressed'.

3   See Landry, 2000 and Chapter 1 of Hall, 1999.

4   The origins of the move towards community or participatory arts in the UK has been written about elsewhere: see for example, Coult and Kershaw, 1990, Itzin, 1980, Kershaw, 1992, Fox, 2002.

5   For a digest of mainly US-based arts education research in this area, see Catterall, Hetland and Winner, 2002; for a study of the 'effects and effectiveness' of arts education in UK secondary schools, see Harland *et al*, 2001.

6   For case studies of these issues from London, see Gardiner and Peggie, 2004. From the USA, these kinds of problems have also been documented by Project Zero in the following publication: Seidel, S., Eppel, M., Martiniello, M. (2001) Arts Survive: A Study of Sustainability in Arts Education Partnerships, Cambridge, MA: Project Zero at the Harvard Graduate School of Education

7   For some examples from the US, see Aprill, Burnaford and Weiss 2001; Simpson, 2002 and Fiske, 1999.

8   There is not space to do justice to this argument within the scope of this book. However, for more detailed discussion of the issues, see Williams, 1959; Stenhouse, 1967; Giroux, 1981; Shils, 1983; hooks, 1989; Middleton, 1990; Shepherd, 1991; Hall and du Gay, 1996; Giroux and Shannon, 1997; Gale and Densmore, 2000.

9   See Tate (1999), explored in Kearney (2003), and Woodhead's strange mix of moral panic and conspiracy theory in *Class War* (2002).

2

NewVIc, a story of the college, its staff and students

Graham Jeffery

The regeneration of Newham: statistics, spectacle and social inclusion

Newham, according to the UK government's most recent assessment, is the fifth most deprived borough in Britain (DETR, 2003). It has one of the UK's lowest proportions of residents with further and higher education qualifications, and certain areas have among the highest unemployment rates in the country. Around a third of the working population have no qualifications. A third of Newham's population are Asian, a fifth are Black or Black British and a third are white British.

Newham has high and rising fertility rates, high teenage pregnancy rates, much higher than average incidence of tuberculosis, cancer and heart disease, the lowest average life expectancy in London, and a high proportion of people living in private rented accommodation. Over half the school aged population have English as an additional language, and 40 percent of children are entitled to free school meals.

This litany of statistics is similar to many inner-city contexts around the world. Clearly Newham Council and the other major agencies tasked with providing services, planning development and supporting the population have serious challenges. London has always been a city of sharp contrasts and inequality, and the 'dual city' (Watson and Bridge, 2002) and social polarisation associated with 'the rise of the highly skilled and paid financial and business and service sector... paralleled by growth of a low paid service sector and the decline of the skilled middle income groups in manufacturing industry' (Hamnett, 2003, p7) brings the issue of who benefits from London's status and economic power as a global city into sharp focus (LDA, 2003; Sassen, 1999, 2001).

Alongside some of the most economically deprived communities in Europe, other communities have sprung up which are characterised by spectacular corporate wealth and global power. On land formerly occupied by factories, warehouses, jetties and freight terminals, where goods and materials arrived from all over the British empire, new informational hubs defined by the flows of international capital have materialised. The regeneration of the Docklands, in particular Canary Wharf and its environs, with its skyscrapers, luxury shopping and housing, an international airport, extensive private security and public surveillance, marinas, restaurants and fitness centres, displays all the paraphernalia of globalised high-rolling living, right next door to extreme poverty.

Since the mid 1990s, Stratford and the so-called 'arc of opportunity' that stretches from the Stratford Rail Lands into the Lower Lea Valley, the main site for London's 2012 Olympic bid, and the vast tracts of vacant land around the Royal Docks have received hundreds of millions of pounds of public money in the form of infrastructural improvements, business development grants, and incentives to private developers and employers to locate there. The many stories of this re-development, with Canary Wharf taking on iconic status as a paradigm of radical corporatist urban regeneration, have been told elsewhere (see, for example Hall, 1999, p888-931; Cohen, 1998; Hamnett, 2003, p228-246). The opportunities, choices and life-chances available to the privileged residents and workers in the Canary Wharf development sit in sharp contrast to the those of the people who service the corporate economy as cleaners, security guards or catering workers. East London's potential as a hub of wealth creation in the international economy throws up enormous tensions between different communities and their interests. The promise of business investment and job creation, indisputably necessary if the residential communities of east London are to prosper, requires inventive and inclusive approaches to regeneration, in which education systems at all levels, from basic skills development to HE, have a crucial role to play (see Gordon, 1996; Butler and Rustin, 1996; Butler, 2000).

In this fast moving and politically charged context, all public sector institutions are continuously performing difficult balancing acts to attract investment, maintain and improve services, and meet the needs and expectations of an extraordinarily diverse range of stakeholders. In 1998, Newham MP Stephen Timms, feeding off the euphoria of the election of the New Labour government, wrote confidently in an article heralding a new wave of initiatives and strategies for the region: 'East London has the most severe problems of urban deprivation to be found anywhere in Britain – but it also presents the most spectacular opportunities for urban regeneration in Europe' (Timms, 1998, p87).

This co-existence of deprivation and spectacle (see Blake and Jeffery, 2001a) makes the transformative promise of culture-led regeneration double edged. On the one hand, culture has an appeal as 'a euphemism for the city's new representation as a creative force in the emerging service economy' (Zukin, 1995, p268), as a means of 'constructing urban images' (Bianchini *et al*, 1993, Harvey, 1989 p233) to attract and retain 'the creative class' (Florida, 2002). On the other hand, if the net effect of this investment, drawing on the multicultural capital and hybridity of the locality and investing heavily in events, cultural activity and improvements to the built environment and streetscape, makes the area so attractive that rents and property values rise to price existing residents, artists and all but the most affluent out of the area, who ultimately benefits (see Smith, 1996; Attfield, 1998)? The unanswered question is how Newham's diverse residential communities are to benefit from these developments, and not simply provide low-cost labour to service a consumption-driven leisure and tourism economy for an affluent minority. For any hope of sustaining social inclusion, culture-led regeneration must pay close attention to the linkages between education, training and entry to employment, understood in broad terms through formal and informal participation in the cultural economy (Blake and Jeffery, 2001a, 2001b; LDA, 2004a).

> Newham offers enormous potential as a place to live and work. It is a thriving area which is undergoing a remarkable transformation – rapidly emerging as a centre of commerce and culture. Situated just three miles from the City, Newham takes in much of London's revitalised docklands, including City Airport, the ExCeL international exhibition centre and luxury homes overlooking the Thames... It's not just the shining new buildings and facilities that make the borough a happening place. Newham has the youngest and most diverse population in the UK... All of which makes for an exciting area rich in colour, flavour and atmosphere where local people take great pride in being part of a global village. The borough's youthful vigour and creativity has fused with the traditional East End values of warmth, friendliness, community spirit and good humour to make New-

ham a welcoming place with a unique character. (www.newham.gov.uk/
aboutus/discover.htm – accessed 24th July 2004)

Where the diversity and vibrancy of local communities is being sold hard as
a cultural asset to prospective investors, educational institutions and
cultural organisations are charged with a *mediating* role. If the communities of Newham are to participate fully in the opportunities presented
by the new economies of East London, rapid skills development, signi-
ficantly improved qualification levels, and major investment in support for
new and existing small businesses are required. At the opening ceremony
for the University of East London's new Docklands campus, celebrated
urbanist Professor Peter Hall commented pessimistically that 'it will take at
least two generations to sort out re-skilling and adapting working class
labourist culture to the new economy of East London; there is a profound
and almost unbridgeable gap between the old and new economy' (author's
notes).

In fact, through a sustained improvement in qualifications obtained, and in
participation and attendance rates at all levels, education systems in
Newham are generally performing well. The University of East London has
seen an improvement in admissions, retention and degree completions
and is one of the leading institutions in widening participation in entry to
higher education in the UK. Half of its students are mature students and
over 60 percent are from ethnic minority groups. Measured in the performative terms of inspection reports and statistics, which inevitably paint
only a partial picture of the effectiveness of institutions, schools and
colleges in Newham are generally regarded as making significant progress
in raising the attainment of young people. The last inspection of NewVIc in
2000 yielded a high grade profile, with no curriculum area being graded at
less than 2 (good) and the arts and media curriculum area 1 (outstanding)
(FEFC, 2000). The most recent inspection of Newham LEA by Ofsted(2003c,
p7) noted that:

> pupils' attainment is below the national average at all key stages. However
> there are good rates of improvement, both against national trends and
> similar authorities. Performance becomes closer to national norms as
> pupils progress through the key stages, and by Key Stage 4 performance is
> close to the national average. This is a powerful indication of the value
> added by the schools.

The Newham Youth and Community Education Service (NEWCEYS) runs
flourishing after school programmes, summer schools and adult education
classes with high participation levels across the borough. Hundreds of

voluntary sector organisations undertake vital work across the spectrum of learning, from basic skills to business support. And there is an increasing emphasis on dialogue, partnership and linked programmes of work between these sectors.

The college curriculum: contexts and histories

When the college opened in 1992, only around 25 percent of the borough's students were leaving school with four passes at GCSE grade C or above. So a traditional sixth form curriculum, in which entry was selected by prior achievement and the curriculum was built around A-Levels was not an option. A decision was taken to offer one-year intermediate vocational qualifications (GNVQ Intermediates and BTEC First Diplomas) rather than GCSE resits (apart from Maths and English Language) as a different kind of educational experience for students who had not succeeded within the GCSE framework. Around a third of the students in the college are enrolled on Level 2 (GCSE equivalent) intermediate vocational programmes. Over the twelve years of the college's life, staff have become accustomed to an almost continuous revision of the qualification framework for 14-19 year old students[1], and with the outcome of the Tomlinson review due in late 2004 we are bracing ourselves for further shifts in the framework.

The rapid growth in the priority given to vocational education within the UK education system from the mid 1980s on was driven by several contradictory impulses. In part it took the form of a response to what Kathryn Ecclestone (2002, p10) characterises as a 'crisis of exclusion', which was very marked in East London. In 1992, most young people in Newham left school with hardly any usable qualifications, and the local labour market was restructuring so rapidly that the forms of apprenticeship, casual and manual work and informal employment on which many young working class people had historically relied were evaporating. The new college tried to construct a curriculum that would be motivating, relevant and tailored to the needs of students pursuing higher education or employment, based upon optimism about what young people could achieve.

Another impulse behind the introduction of a more extensive framework of vocational qualifications was the business ideologies which dominated the Conservative government's thinking. The fracture in the educational Right's thinking between a narrow market-led vocationalism in which education was essentially about preparedness for the job market (see, for example CBI, 1989, 1993), and a rigid insistence on the 'gold standard' of the traditional academic curriculum have been well documented (see for example

Young, 1998; Ball, 2001). In the formation of the NewVIc 'comprehensive' curriculum for 16-19 year olds, there was an attempt to strike a balance between a very broad A-Level offer and a wide range of vocational opportunities.

The take-up of vocational qualifications, despite the government's intention in 1993 that they would be a substantial part of the curriculum for all 16-19 year olds, has been highly differentiated between the different parts of the post-16 sector (see Ecclestone, 2002). With the move towards another new formula for the 14-19 curriculum, the status of vocational learning has probably never been higher. But there are still fundamental fractures in attitudes and approaches to teaching, learning and assessment across different parts of the system, and between the different qualification frameworks, which inhibit wider embedding of 'critical vocational' practices[2], such as are described in this book.

There are marked differences between patterns of provision in school sixth forms and the further education sector as a whole. Even within the sixth form college sector there is immense variation in the level of selectiveness and the range of qualifications on offer. There is also an ongoing question about whether secondary schools are currently equipped to develop the appropriate infrastructure and resources to support large scale vocational learning programmes. One solution being proposed through such initiatives as the DfES's 14-19 'pathfinder' programmes (DfES, 2003) is to bring greater coherence to the pathways and choices available in the 14-19 sector. The Learning and Skills Councils are charged with working closely with LEAs, head teachers and college principals to plan collaboratively for 14-19 provision, and have generated numerous shared projects, intra-organisational programmes and partnership meetings. Employers, the Connexions careers guidance agencies, lifelong learning services, the community and voluntary sector, and a host of other economic development and regeneration agencies are all intended to have a stake in this process too.

Inclusive teaching and learning

The starting point of the college was that it would be inclusive. Sid Hughes' vision for the college was that it would be run on democratic lines – but not that 'the person who shouts the loudest always gets what they want' (interview, 2002). Although the college is noted for its informal and friendly atmosphere, there are strong administrative and pastoral systems in place to ensure that all students are supported.

> It's a very simple thing if you say, if you genuinely believe the student ought to be at the centre of the organisation, then it informs most of what you do, it informs you about the recruitment process, it informs the way in which you teach, it informs the way you assess students, and the way you behave with students. (interview transcript, 2002).

The college's first prospectus made the approach to students and their learning clear:

> To be accepted at the college there is one important entry qualification. You must be determined to achieve. This could be at A-level or on a vocational course leading directly to future career opportunities. But it could equally be coming to grips with an individual challenge improving language, numeracy or physical and creative skills. What we expect from you is a belief in yourself, a willingness to learn with others and a determination to succeed. What we will provide you with are the necessary resources and the quality of teaching and support to help you achieve your ambitions. (NewVIc, 1992)

As a new institution, it rapidly had to forge an identity, build working relationships and develop a distinct and purposeful agenda. Before the opening of the college, post-16 provision in Newham was uncoordinated. Participation was low and based mainly on traditional A-level modes. A large college of further education catered for vocational learning, but there was no clear focus on post-16 progression or the appropriateness or coherence of the curriculum. The LEA took a politically courageous decision to close all the school sixth forms, except for a denominational sixth form attached to two voluntary-aided Catholic secondary schools, and concentrate provision on a new site with a new build college.

Governmental rhetoric founded on market models, and the newly minted, centralised National Curriculum did not favour experimentation, collaboration or partnership. However, a focus on the development of vocational qualifications alongside A-level provision, linked to Newham's track record in defending comprehensive education and pioneering integrated and inclusive education for students with physical and learning disabilities, meant that a college based on comprehensive principles and inclusive learning could be founded without too much ideological debate.

The college became incorporated and formally separated from the LEA as a result of the 1992 Education Act. Like other institutions such as Stantonbury Campus in Milton Keynes, which controversially exploited some of the freedoms the quasi-independence of Grant Maintained Status offered so as to maintain a distinct and radical identity in the face of government and LEA hostility, NewVIc insisted on innovative approaches as the best means of responding to the challenges of the urban context. It did not want to be like school; it wanted to mark a fresh start for learners. From the start, the college cultivated an informal atmosphere and emphasised honest relationships, symbolised by the use of first names between students and staff. This ethos was combined with high levels of investment in new technologies and learning resources.

The college emphasised parity of esteem between academic and vocational routes. Its extensive offer of vocational qualifications alongside A-levels was highly unusual for a sixth form college in 1992. Growth was rapid. NewVIc now has over 2,100 full time students aged 16-19, 700 part time adult students and 150 students enrolled on a range of higher education courses delivered in partnership with the University of East London. Exam results across all programmes have consistently been at or above national averages, even though the GCSE grade profile on entry of the students is amongst the lowest of any sixth form college in the country, and student retention is high: 80 percent for level 2 programmes and 89 percent for level 3 programmes in 2002-3. Whilst these figures are around average for sixth form colleges nationally, the intake profile of the students resembles an inner-city general FE college more than the largely selective sixth form colleges on which the national benchmarks for achievement for such colleges are based.

Behind the headline of solid achievement in terms of qualifications gained are a number of important stories about the ways in which formal and informal approaches to learning have been woven together.

Learning communities and inclusion

A major feature of the college's ethos from its beginnings was an emphasis on teaching quality, and it provided leadership in approaches to teaching and learning. There was openness to new approaches, and a willingness to explore different ways of doing things.

> We had to be open enough to look for creative solutions. And having creative people around was vitally important, and having teams that were creative in their approaches: we didn't want all teams to teach in exactly the same way. We do know, and everybody I think would sit round a table and agree, what the sort of fundamental basic requirements for good teaching are, but how those might be interpreted at subject level is for us all to work on. And there was also the related idea, that let's have a curriculum which is sufficiently varied and flexible for people to be able to choose from a whole range of different things; they might not know that they want to do

them when they come in, but once they're here they will see all these things going on. (Sid Hughes, interview transcript, 2002)

Hughes refers to the notion of a learning community or learning culture: a socially constructed base of values or ways of doing things that people grow into and come to take as a 'way of life' (Hodkinson *et al*, 1996; Ecclestone, 2002, p171). A key attraction for staff and students was to be part of a new environment, in which there were high quality resources, and learning spaces that were fit for purpose.

Learning support and tutoring were given high priority. Every full time member of the teaching staff had responsibility for a tutor group, which they saw for two hours per week in a Supported Studies session. A planning framework and a curriculum for Supported Studies has evolved which, whilst linked to a common framework of activities across the college involving action planning, careers planning, ICT training, and study skills support, also provides sufficient time for tutors to work with their students as individuals and develop a climate of peer support (see Chapter 3). Underpinning this is a clear commitment:

If a student wants to come here and do A-level mathematics, for example, but they happen to be blind, well, then we have to make sure they can do mathematics by making sure that they have access to all the resources they need to do A-level mathematics. You don't say: actually, this person's a bit of a risk and I'd like to pass because they're blind. The person wants to do maths because they've got the qualification to do it: you have to support that student. What is true in that fairly obvious way because it's a very physical requirement, is also true across the board.

You have to be patient. You have to go the distance with students rather than assume that every time there's a problem that they can't do this course and you back off and say 'you can't do that'... you've got a disability, you're blind... what people put in the way of the students performing we would try to challenge and see if the student could be supported.

So we put... a lot of work into [developing] student services, but also ... every person who was a teacher would be a tutor, the tutoring would be on the timetable; it would be compulsory. You have to realise this is a time when tutoring was a sort of, it was a nominal thing in most colleges. You would be a tutor but you would never actually meet your tutor group. You'd have one to one type meetings with tutees when they turned up but you didn't actually run a full tutorial programme.

We recognised that... if we were genuinely concerned about students of all abilities you had to realise that students would come with different support needs, they couldn't all just be taught the same... And neither could you determine what that support would be because some of it might be personal guidance or support, or it might be academic... And so to invest so heavily in student support systems and resources, that made the college much... more inclusive even in the early stages than most other colleges around it. And that was a real struggle. (Hughes, interview transcript, 2002)

From the outset, the college sought additional funding beyond that provided by core government grants. It has managed to accumulate a surplus for every year of operation by avoiding a hierarchical staffing structure with many managers, or allocating much remission from contact time for those with additional responsibilities. It ran large groups of students in most subject areas, and emphasised efficiency.

Evolving a collaborative model

Responsibility for leading programmes was given directly to teaching teams co-ordinated by managers. And a number of staff used the relatively sophisticated support structure to find ways of developing partnerships with external agencies, organisations and individuals who could add value to the core curriculum. Jacqui Mace, who worked as a development manager for the college from 1992 to 2003, explained why she thought performing arts and media teachers, in particular, worked so successfully in partnership:

> ...because performance and media involves looking outwards and the results of their work can be shared publicly; and also, in the early days, this was a relatively beleaguered area of work for the college, in the sense that it wasn't recruiting well. The team had good resources but low recruitment, particularly in the performing arts. So they had to find ways of getting students involved, and they used projects and partnerships to do it. (interview transcript, 2002)

A mindset began to evolve which saw the curriculum design as a form of research and artistic practice. Clare Connor, who joined the college as a teacher of dance in 1996 and played a leading role in developing the partnership-based curriculum and networks of practice, commented

> From my work with Union Dance as a dancer, I'd been up and down the country, doing different kinds of arts education residencies. I knew that there were different ways of being in the school as an artist other than the single, one off workshop and I'd seen some FE colleges such as Swindon or Darlington that were experimenting with this approach. I had been working at Islington Green School and had developed a number of projects in partnership with Education and Community Programmes at the The Place there, and also City and Islington College, and seen the impact on the

students... I'd done my homework about east London and had thought about the other agencies and partners that NewVIc could work with, and at interview I emphasised this. Also, a key moment for me when I was doing my training at London Contemporary Dance School was that we had Janet Archer leading a session (who now runs Dance City in Newcastle) and she really challenged the idea that 'those who can't, teach' – a penny dropped for me. (interview transcript, 2004)

Triche Kehoe, teacher of drama, who had also worked as an actor and was part of the team from the start, recalled 'the idea of teacher as practitioner, as having their own artistic practice to inform their work in the classroom was always really important, and we could present that in the language of 'up to date industrial experience' which had currency at the time' (interview transcript, 2003). A case could be made that partnership working and direct work with cultural organisations was a form of intrinsic and peer-supported professional development. The development of the BTEC curriculum in art and design, media and performing arts in the late 80s and early 90s was an early example of a 'creative industries' approach, in which business values influenced arts education. Many staff in the Art, Design and Media teams had backgrounds in film, graphic design and other aspects of the creative industries.

Principles for curriculum design were established:

- to look outside the walls of the college for ways of connecting with the communities the college serves, to establish broader contexts for learning

- to try to render learning at the college meaningful in the context of the experiences, interests and pre-existing knowledge base of the students

- to connect with the communities that the learners come from and to use locations other than the college as sites for learning

- to make use of the professional, artistic and industrial skills of the teaching team in the construction of the curriculum, which develops motivation in staff and models of apprenticeship for learners

- to draw upon the expertise and knowledge of cultural and artistic partners in the construction of the curriculum

Successful bids for regeneration funding, mostly written by the teachers themselves, expanded the team's activities. This funded administrators and short and long-term project managers, who worked alongside the teachers. These people were appointed because of their specialist skills and experience in arts management rather than general administration, and without them the projects could never have been sustained. Project funding also allowed the staffing to expand more rapidly than if the college had simply introduced new full-time learning programmes. As Sid Hughes put it: 'project funding has been a major driver of innovation' (internal consultation document, 2004).

The team began to make the college's spaces and facilities available for the wider community. There were Saturday morning classes, free access to rehearsal and production spaces for visiting companies and artists, and alliances with producing organisations that used the college as a venue, working with the Greenwich and Docklands International Festival and East London Dance. In 1995 Newham Council began discussing a capital bid for a new Lottery funded arts centre, to be built alongside the Theatre Royal, Stratford East. The story of the college's involvement with Stratford Circus is told in Chapter 6. In the run-up to its opening, the college seconded staff to Stratford Circus. The teachers who were developing these new roles enabled the college to act as a co-producer and commissioner of artistic work – in film, music, theatre and dance. Projects included touring theatre and workshops led by students in local schools, performances as part of the London International Festival of Theatre in 1997 and 1999, co-commissioned international choreographic work performed at Sadlers Wells and The Place, work in sites such as Trinity Buoy Wharf on the River Thames, and in other venues across the city. All this created a virtuous circle within which partnerships began to lever new resources, provide new opportunities and raise the stakes for students and staff by exposing them to new contexts and settings.

The catalytic effect of knowledge and resource sharing with the partner organisations, many of which played a pivotal role in the London's arts sector, created a pool of expertise and information that fed back into the curriculum and built new opportunities. Problems arose when the volume of satellite projects around the core curriculum for 16-19 year olds grew. Skilled teachers had less time for direct work with students in the classroom because they were developing and managing work with schools and regeneration projects or developing artistic programmes in film, theatre, business support or community learning. Tension mounted between the core mission and priorities of the college as set out in its strategic plan, the teachers' job descriptions, and some of the enthusiasms and creative ambitions of members of the team. The volume of work required to maintain the partnerships overtook the rate at which new posts could be introduced. The team debated their job roles and the college's mission: some supported a sharp focus on the delivery of qualifications and classroom-based activity, others advocated a broader, more expansive interpretation (see Chapters 5 and 7).

Internal tensions also developed over hidden hierarchies. Newly-appointed staff were initially deployed in classroom settings for almost all of their time, while others ventured into the new territories of community based learning, creative business support and participatory film-making, theatrical and artistic projects. The volume of information flow and dialogue required to maintain management control of these projects became overwhelming, and the college's information management and administration systems struggled to keep pace with the rate of innovation. Formal and informal professional development strategies were needed to support all staff in developing their creative ambitions and meeting the needs of their students. Managers needed excellent mediation skills, to develop project design and management skills in new staff, and to avoid conflicts of interest and clarify values in the projects.

The core principle – that any new programme or project supported by the college needed to be clearly identified as *student-centred and focused on learner needs* had to be clearly articulated and reiterated. This was emphatically not about teachers doing their own thing but about designing projects which would develop creativity for students and staff, and make a real difference to students' learning. As the team's responsibilities to its partners grew, learners and staff began to become increasingly mobile and to work in other professional or community settings. The number of performing arts students entering higher education also dramatically increased.

Rashpal Singh Bansal

Rashpal Singh Bansal studied performing arts at NewVIc from 1996 to 1999. Having worked with distinguished dance artists whilst still at NewVIc, he began focusing on his own choreographic work. He trained at London Contemporary Dance School before going on to pursue a career in choreography. Bansal has made works for Jerwood Space, Greenwich and Docklands Festivals, Shobana Jeyasingh Dance Company and the Royal Opera House, as well as for his own company, United Dance Artists. Currently he is working with various technologies to develop the multi media applications of his work.

'I went on the BTEC First wanting to be an actor but ended up getting into dance because on the BTEC First Clare Connor introduced me to a new type of dance that I was not familiar with. She got me involved with Wayne MacGregor, Saburo Teshigawara, and Mark Murphy, mostly on a project basis. They were artists who were highly regarded and I was inspired. Wayne MacGregor's company came into the college to do a project over some months between 1996 and 1997, then we made a piece. I didn't know what I was getting myself involved with; you watch it and the dancing is so accomplished and futuristic. That and Saburo at the Queen Elizabeth Hall showed me the different places you can take dance. My view before that was narrow and small, because students that age only see dance as portrayed through TV, the media and as ballet.

The BTEC First and National was fun. It was creative because it gave us the freedom to explore, outside of class time you could do what you want – you could stay on and use the college to do dance if you wanted, or you could go home, go out at lunch break or stay at college. There was a profound amount of freedom outside of the course.

There are colleges that focus on technique but NewVIc never aspired to do that. The BTEC courses focused on the academic side of dance – the history behind it, some great dancers and on making dance. What is great about being 17 is that you have an enormous amount of untapped confidence so you can just be yourself when you work with the highly regarded artists who you work with on the projects. At 25 it's different as you can be intimidated by them by then.

At 17 you are like a sponge and all they [the teachers] did was turn on the tap and I just absorbed it. The most important thing I got from NewVIc was my development in the spiritual sense, in my artistic development. I definitely can't do justice to how great an impact it had on where I am now. I was going to do acting – I wouldn't have tried dance.

Clare got me involved with anything she thought might be beneficial to my development and guided me through my experiences. I always thought the students were treated as artists, spoken with and worked with intellectually. I always felt that that was the way they treated us. The teachers didn't put expectations on you. It meant we felt free to explore as artists.' (interview transcript, 2004)

Vertical learning and additionality

Two important principles emerged that set the work of the arts and media team apart from some of the other teams at NewVIc. The first was the expanding use of what came to be called vertical learning through projects: the idea that by developing learning frameworks in which people of different ages and with different experiences work together, dialogue is opened up which creates new possibilities for students and requires them to question their attitudes, values and motivation, and to behave more responsibly. Many of the most successful projects were based on encounters between young people and significant others who brought an outsider's view to the learning situation.

For example, between 1997 and 2000 the three *Shift* integrated dance, design and music projects, brokered by East London Dance and led by Lucy Moelwyn Hughes, Tom St Louis and Jackie Sands, brought together adults with physical disabilities from a local community centre with 17 and 18-year old BTEC National performing arts students. The outcomes of the projects were artistically startling[3]; they also springboarded a host of other developments, including the development of the integrated HND in performing arts, and more and more mobility impaired and visually impaired students studying performing arts at NewVIc. Other projects worked extensively with young people from partner primary and secondary schools and involved them in mentoring and vertical relationships with students, teachers and artists. The expanding web of relationships with arts organisations offered numerous opportunities for student placements and staff development and began to build pathways for progression into employment and further learning – for the staff as well as the students.

This led to the second important principle, which the team expanded beyond college norms: the notion of 'core' and 'additional' learning opportunities. All students enrolled on full time programmes in performing arts and media have an entitlement that will include work with professional artists and at least one extended project in a community setting. And woven around this core entitlement is a set of additional projects, classes and workshops in the arts, funded through money brought in from a diverse range of additional sources and through ongoing relationships with partner organisations. Through engagement with these ongoing and ever-changing projects, students can choose their own pathways based on their needs and interests and enhance their core learning with a wide range of additional studies, some accredited, some not. The open access principle followed by the college means that students are positively encouraged to book resources out, rehearse independently, and develop their own projects and initiatives. In effect, a wider cultural infrastructure has been developed to support the curriculum which allows staff and students to access opportunities beyond the confines of the institution.

Summary: a connected curriculum

Beyond the further education curriculum for 500 full time 16-19 year old learners in the arts and media team, a considerably extended offer in the performing arts and media has grown up:

- Three degree level programmes delivered as a collaboration with the School of Social Science, Media and Cultural Studies at the University of East London, now with over 120 HE students enrolled

  i.   BA (Hons) Performing Arts (Community Development) and HND Performing Arts in the Community

  ii. BA (Hons) Music Culture: theory and production

  iii. Extended degree programme in Creative and Cultural Industries

- Circus Media creative business support service, managed by the College but based at Stratford Circus, and delivered as a partnership with the resident organisations there, now incorporating a Centre of Vocational Excellence in digital and broadcast media (see Chapter 6)

- An Arts in Health programme based at Stratford Circus working across sectors and communities

- Professional development programmes for artists and creative professionals, including *People Moving*, a one-day training programme in integrated dance practice, and, launched in Spring 2005, the *Teacher-Artist Partnership* qualification with a consortium of London arts and education organisations

- Work with schools and the wider community and a wide ranging additional learning programme which includes regular classes, workshops, summer schools and special projects, mostly delivered in partnership.

- A significant strategic role in the arrangements for the management, administration and planning for the Stratford Circus performing arts centre

Consequently, teaching staff juggle multiple roles: between work in schools and communities, between teaching in further and higher education, between project management, artistic leadership, and research and development. There are serious issues to be resolved if this model is to be sustained. But for learners this provides a uniquely complex and rich landscape which enables rapid mobility between different settings, spaces and programmes – in which, it could be argued, 'zones of proximal development' (Vygotsky, 1978) and 'legitimate peripheral participation' (Lave, 1991) are built into the design of learning experiences for students.

Beyond the academic/vocational divide?

The vision statement of the arts team, drawn up in 1999 to summarise a lively team meeting by curriculum manager Paul Wakeling, read as follows:

> Arts and Leisure is a student centred team that believes in the abilities of its students. Our students can achieve at least as well as students anywhere else in the country. To do this our students may need extra support which we are ready to give. We aim to ensure that the students fulfil their potential while they are at NewVIc and we also aim to ensure that they progress to do appropriate and fulfilling courses or work when they leave.
>
> We believe that our students benefit from genuinely vocational training and we would like to give them an education with genuine connections with the world of work. This includes maintaining connections with industry and working with up to date hardware and software that is industry standard. We are committed to keeping our resources up to date and keeping our staff trained to teach the use of the equipment.
>
> The academic and vocational divide is a false divide and our A Level students are entitled to work on project work that utilises our best vocational practice, equipment and industry links. Vocational students are encouraged to take academic qualifications and A Level students will be encouraged to take Vocational Units.
>
> Our team does not exist in isolation but as part of a college and part of the wider community. It is our aim to provide a cultural service to the college and the community, to aim to enrich the college and community through our work. We also aim to provide well balanced, skilled and qualified people for the local job market. It is our aim that good and appropriate jobs in Newham go to students from NewVIc, before or after university.
>
> The arts, sport, tourism and cultural industries are at the heart of the regeneration strategies for our region. By providing realistic opportunities for our students to engage in project work with outside agencies, work experience, visits, and direct contact with industry professionals we will equip them with the skills required to make the most of these emerging opportunities. The challenges of new technologies, new media, flexible employment patterns and social and economic deprivation must inform our work at every level. Our curriculum is broader than just what happens at NewVIc; it relates and responds to the local cultural context and it engages

with partners to drive forward the regeneration of the local economy. In working with our partners, we will develop the profile of the College as a key educational resource for the borough, and we will help Newham's young people to achieve their full potential in the next century.

Such autonomous ways of working are facilitated by the flexible informational and physical architecture of the college and its extensive use of vocational qualifications. The team has emphasised flexibility and innovation within the structure of the qualification framework – since the structure and content of national qualification frameworks largely determine the parameters within which teachers in FE can work – but it also stresses the climate in which these frameworks and contents are delivered. This is an atmosphere of dialogue, encouragement and achievement, in which the formal and informal aspects of learning are woven together. A learning culture for the arts.

Notes

1   For some of the bones of this process see Finegold *et al*, 1990; DfEE, 1997; CBI, 1989, 1993; Young, 1998; Hodgson and Spours, 1999.

2   Young, 1998, p56: 'The principles of critical vocationalism would give priority to the ways that young people can relate to work and knowledge and how they can draw on both subject knowledge and their experience and understanding of work in developing their ideas about the future. It would draw on academic subjects to shed light on the social divisions and changes in the current organisation of work and draw on the work experience of students to help give meaning and context to subject-based knowledge'.

3   A short film of the *Shift 2* project is available to view at www.newvic-creative.org.uk

3

The BTEC First Diploma in Performing Arts

Kelly Davidson and Rachel Fell

This chapter summarises key findings from a one-year ethnographic study examining the dynamics of teaching and learning for a group of BTEC First Diploma Performing Arts students.

Nearly one-third of the 2,100 full time students aged 16-19 at New VIc are on intermediate (Level 2) programmes which act as a fresh start for those that have not achieved the four Cs at GCSE required for progression onto an advanced (level 3) programme – either at A-level or through vocational A-levels or BTEC National qualifications. We focused on a particular group of students studying for a BTEC First Diploma (BFD) in Performing Arts.

The BFD is a full time, one-year programme. Students take units in Dance, Drama, Music and the Performing Arts Business. The students also have opportunities to perform in and outside of the college, at Stratford Circus and elsewhere, and take part in other projects and professional workshops. The course is delivered through extended projects, often involving more than one member of staff, and combining several units of study as specified by the accrediting body Edexcel. Students' performance is assessed in relation to specific competences or learning outcomes set out in units of study. A wide variety of skills are assessed, from written and research based work to practical performance. There is little formal testing or time-limited assessment tasks performed under examination conditions. Rather, the programme aims to develop vocational skills in contexts which are as close as possible to industrial conditions.

Performing arts disciplines are regarded by the teaching team as a vehicle for the overall development of the students' performance in future professional life. The language of employability and vocational relevance is interpreted more broadly than simply training for job roles in the creative industries: it provides a framework within which values of professional conduct and skills can be developed in performance, self-management and communication.

Successful learning in the performing arts requires the acquisition of skills of teamwork, problem solving, effective communication and empathy. The gradual development of student awareness of the diversity of learning styles and life stories of other students in the group establishes a more confident and risk-taking learning climate.

Beyond the reference to employability and training for the performing arts industry, common to vocational education everywhere, the NewVIc course has been engineered by the teaching team to allow students to learn the life skill of peer support. It means that the group become dependent on and increasingly supportive of each other, unlike traditional educational models where they depend on the teacher. They are assessed on their individual performance, usually based on the application of relatively abstracted skills and knowledge, under formalised conditions. This shift is achieved through team teaching, making use of a particular model of learning support assistant/learning support artist (LSA), and co-teaching with professional artists from outside the college.

The course has been structured on the principles of power sharing with students, and dialogue, on the lines of Paulo Freire's 'education for transformation' (Freire, 1998a). One of the BFD students said she had enjoyed the year especially because of 'the way you see people transform, personalities changing'. Teachers are aware of the limits of their authority; and the contractual nature of the relationship between students and teachers is different to that of school because the students have made a deliberate choice to attend this course. But many of these learners have relatively limited choices post-16 because of their low self-confidence and poor GCSE grades and, in many instances, challenging home circumstances. This is essentially an intermediary year designed to help the transition between school and a more adult approach to education. The objective is to help individuals to grow and develop as learners.

Student body of 2002-3

The BFD group of 2002-3 was broadly reflective of the ethnic diversity of the borough, except that, like many other performing arts programmes, Asian students were under-represented proportionally. At the start and end of the programme the ethnic profile of the group was as follows:

	First PA %		successful completion	Achievement: % of starters
Asian Indian	1	3.57	1	100%
Asian Pakistani	1	3.57	1	100%
Black African	8	28.57	6	75%
Black Caribbean	3	10.7	3	100%
Black Other	1	3.57	1	100%
Mixed White/Asian	1	3.57	1	100%
White British	8	28.57	4	50%
Any Other	3	14.28	2	66%
Not Known	1	3.57	1	100%
Total	**27**		**20**	**74%**

Research has consistently shown that African Caribbean, Pakistani and Bangladeshi young people to underachieve in schools. But there is no essentialist correlation between ethnic origin and predicted achievement. Studies have shown that identity is constructed across many different parameters, in relation to language, culture, gender, geographies and histories (see, for example, Cohen, 1996, 1998; Brice-Heath and McLaughlin, 1993; Ball *et al*, 2000). The task of an education institution in this context of shifting and multiplying differences – with students continually negotiating between narratives of poverty and disadvantage and narratives of opportunity and access to resources – is to enable and facilitate young people in their navigation across these landscapes of difference. The BFD course is one of the most successful intermediate programmes in the college, with student achievement and retention over the last eight years consistently exceeding national averages for intermediate programmes. In 2002, retention for the programme was recorded at 74 per cent, lower than in previous years. The ethnic group with the lowest achievement and retention rate were white

British students. Twelve female and fifteen male students started the pro-gramme. Nine female and eleven male students completed it.

Integrated research
Our study used the existing framework of the college's Supported Studies curriculum.

Supported studies, with self-reflection and evaluation built into its core structure, is ideally suited to the action research framework that we developed – it became just another dimension to the year's activity. We found that the research was helpful for these students' learning and development as it allowed them extended and structured opportunities to talk about their experiences and reflect on them.

In the case study, we follow six exemplar students. They span the range of background, ability, achievement of intermediate students joining the course each year. We selected this sample group to gain a picture of the diversity of needs, experiences and aspirations of the student body. We had not met them, but based our selection on their application forms, personal and teacher statements. All names are fictitious.

All 20 students who completed the course passed. Seven students left the programme during the year for various reasons: some decided to withdraw, while others followed the advice of their tutors. Three out of the six in our sample group withdrew from the course before the end of the year.

An informal learning climate

The group spent much of the time in the first class of the year joking about getting over the use of first names. A rapport was established between Kelly, their personal tutor, and the students in this game of establishing the level they were now at and this joking/levelling time seemed to suggest how their group relationship would develop. Although Kelly was at the front of the classroom, taking the authority role, the desks were arranged in a U shape, indicating that there is structure in place but equality amongst the learners.

The negotiation of the teacher and students' first meeting is all important. This was where Kelly asserted 'this is what I expect in my classes'. This was done in negotiation with the students, who were asked to consider what they expected from each other.

The careful way the teacher-student relationship was set up on day one was important in shaping how the students would relate to the teachers from then on. The students who were reluctant to address the teacher by her first name were those who had reported negative experiences in their previous education.

Investing time in the students during the induction period is crucial to the motivation, retention and development of the group. The teacher's approach raised students' self-esteem immediately, and helped secure a safe learning environment. The nurturing of the students over the first six weeks is central to the structure of the course; it is essential for the intermediate students who are starting their studies over again, replacing the GCSEs they failed to achieve.

Course design

BTEC students are given a voice because of the flexibility of the course. It is unlike, for example A-levels, in which approaches to teaching and learning are much more constrained by the form and content of assessment tasks and limited timetabled contact. Whereas A-level programmes expected students to work independently and take initiative, staff reported that the BFD programme was regarded as a very 'high dependency' course; students needed intensive support to work on tasks outside of class time. Some arrive with a relatively positive perception of formal education and school, but the majority tend to have negative associations with classroom-based learning. Many have severe problems with written communication, the dominant mode of assessment in school.

The teachers encourage the students to take dance and drama, despite the assessment being in only one of the two. This is to encourage keeping options open. Sometimes a student enters who has no interest in either and then shows a flair for one or the other. Students also need proficiency in both to enjoy the BTEC National, the two year advanced course to which the majority of students will progress.

During the induction phase, professional artists are invited in to give workshops and perform. So students get a taste of live performance from the outset. Having exposure to professional performance work in the first few weeks of their year means that students experience the college and professionals working together right away.

Attention is given to the students' personal interests and potential. Teachers develop some awareness of the home life of students by getting to know them a little; the first day involves introducing your neighbour, sharing information about who they live with – brothers, sisters, pets etc. Each exercise serves multiple purposes. For example, the initial exercise on names helped the course tutor understand a little about each student's preferences and strengths in communication.

By mid year the BFD group are performing their music concert in the space where they have seen professionals performing in the college. Shortly after, they perform their piece in Stratford Circus, where they saw a professional show a few months earlier.

The critical features for the success of this programme design include:

- long blocks of time – no session except ICT is less than two hours long

- extensive use of professional artists and visiting professional companies integrated into main programme delivery

- curriculum topics carefully selected to respond to students' interests and experience, e.g. featuring popular and youth culture, drawing on artists from east London, working across a range of cultural forms and traditions

- strong ongoing communication between members of the teaching team, with daily informal dialogue about students' needs and regular formal meetings

- flexibility of delivery: adjusting time and space – inside and outside the college – and resources according to project needs and student needs

A sense of positive group dynamic is vital. Considerable time and energy is spent establishing and maintaining a positive working atmosphere within the group. Techniques used by teachers to achieve this include:

- emphasising learner autonomy in the discourse of learning: the language of rights and responsibilities is central to the programme from the start.

- the language of ownership is extensively used – students are required to confront their own behaviour and attitudes to their work.

- the phrase 'professional attitude' is repeatedly emphasised by all the teachers

Over the year, there was evidence of students increasingly taking responsibility for and ownership of their studies. However, this is a fragile dynamic and requires constant intervention and maintenance from staff.

The BFD curriculum is organised into extended projects. They range in length from a few days to as long as a whole term, so that the development of outcomes over different scales of time can be experienced, from short, intensive projects to long-term development of performances. There is an emphasis on building relationships between drama, dance and music, and not specialising in any of them. Options are intended to be kept open: many students came in with little interest in one art form but the ongoing relationship between disciplines inspired their interest in another – often to their surprise.

What do students need for success?

■ *To be listened to and respected*

Calling teachers by their first name was singled out as being the first significant shift in life as a student at NewVIc compared with life at school. This was the main reason they gave for why they felt different immediately, alongside their new freedom from school uniform, for which school was remembered as 'strict' and 'restrictive'.

In baseline interviews many of the students told us that their schooling experience had been unfair to them. They had not felt helped, so came to feel that they had been let down in their education so far. Their previous teachers had not shown them respect. Two of the case study students talked about experiences of not being trusted or given the benefit of the doubt. Simon said the worst thing about his schooling was being wrongly accused of something and never being able to clear his name.

Other things the students noticed immediately and appreciated about being a student at college were: the casual dress of both staff and students; friendly staff and smiling faces; being 'treated like adults'; feeling understood; people listening to them; having chosen to be there; 'great facilities', and the building's clean and modern spaces. On the atmosphere in the college, they remarked:

Abdul: 'It's not so strict compared to school. We're calling the teachers by their first names. You don't feel that they have so much authority on you.'

Simon: '...it feels strange but I like it that way. Calling the teachers by their first name makes me feel like I'm not a little boy anymore. At my old school the teachers were rude and we had to call them Miss or Sir.'

Niamh didn't enjoy school, partly because 'It wasn't nice. The teachers were rude. They didn't help you out unless you asked. They were strict, we called them Miss.'

Sasha: 'I hated my school because the teachers were bitches, they gave me not much support, and it was a strict school very different to here. You don't get treated like you're stupid or anything here so it's alright.'

Jessica: 'That school was a joke. Children did whatever they wanted to, it needed more discipline. I would not take my child to that school, that's for sure.'

■ *To have opportunities to develop their own creative ideas, inside and outside the formal curriculum – to have access to informal learning and resources so that they can make their own pathways*

The team provides opportunities for students to access resources beyond the timetabled curriculum – whether to rehearse independently, use music workstations or through additional activities, such as youth drama, youth dance, and music workshops. Students are encouraged to make use of the college as a resource for their personal development as well as to undertake accredited learning. One ex-BFD student who had been with the college for three years commented 'it's because they encourage you to do what you can do and give you access to equipment – then you respect them more because they let you do your thing. They always help.'

■ *To be challenged and supported*

Methods of teaching and learning that are participatory and encompass a wide range of modes of learning: practical, kinaesthetic, aural, visual, oral, written etc. Formal and informal mentoring and apprenticeship are also a key feature of the programme design.

Support and mentoring

College wide support is made up of a student services centre, a college wide youth worker, an open access person-centred counsellor and a Skills Centre where students can obtain help outside of timetabled time with assignments and with literacy and numeracy skills. Teachers in each area were encouraging and commented whenever students showed any new ability or change in behaviour.

Mez: 'I'd heard from people that it was a really good college, for if you needed help you could always get it... it has been like that, from Kelly or from other teachers. The teachers [are what I like best about this college] because if you need help they will say 'I will help you" (mid year interview). The network of support for teachers as well as students is highly visible. The students see that teachers need peers too.

Alex completed the course but decided not to study performing arts further. On reflection about the year he said:

> At the beginning of the year I thought I had made a mistake doing the course... after about two weeks it got better... because Kelly started encouraging me, she kept saying it's going to be OK, she kept on pushing me, kept on saying don't worry... then about half way into the course I felt different about it and that's when it got much better... because of the support from a teacher.' (exit interview)

The group identified the Learning Support Assistants (LSAs) as the second group of people most supportive to them. LSAs at NewVIc are considered to be key to student development. Performing arts trained LSAs were not seen as teachers, nor as learners. In the dance sessions some of the students talked about how they felt encouraged by having a LSA who is also an ex-student. Through observation it appeared that the LSA had a positive effect not only for the student she was supporting with writing and movement, but upon the whole group around her.

Sasha, a student who did not have an LSA allocated to her, was focused and attentive in classes in which an LSA was present. In classes without an LSA she was distracted and lacked concentration. So the presence of the LSA created a better learning environment for the whole group. We suggest that this was not because the LSA was working across the group, or specifically with more than one individual, but because having an ex-student sitting amongst the group and taking it seriously had a positive impact. Sasha observed how the LSA was instructing the student she was with; she seemed to appreciate being able to watch and listen to the guidance the LSA gave to the allocated student (source: researcher diary).

We suggest that the provision of a role model – a teacher, an artist, a peer, or a 'near peer' such as an LSA – can help the fostering of creativity in students (see also Craft, 2003; Lave, 1991).

Laura-Anne Smith, LSA to the BTEC First group 2002-3

Laura-Anne studied at NewVIc between 1999 and 2002. She undertook the BTEC First Diploma in performing arts, then went on to complete the BTEC National in Performing Arts and gained a high grade in A-Level Dance. During her final year Laura was chosen as lead dancer in a NewVIc additional learning project – the film *Home* (see Chapter 4). Over the year East London Dance, the dance development agency for East London, also saw her performance and asked if she would perform in a piece with CandoCo Dance Company. Following that, Laura became assistant choreographer and dancer in a Bollywood film and site specific performance commissioned by East London Dance. She is also employed as a sessional dance tutor at Stratford Circus and in other settings.

Through her professional experience with CandoCo Laura became interested in the role of the LSA. She applied to be attached as an LSA to higher education courses at the University of East London, and worked in that role with two students she knew who had progressed from NewVIc. Since 2002 she has been working as LSA both at NewVIc and UEL.

Laura supported one of the students in the case study group who had behavioural problems. She said the benefits of the role meant that '[Tamina] was calmer... because we would talk together at the beginning of the class she was very energetic and flirty with the boys, by talking she would get her personal stuff out of the way at the beginning, and then she was ready to learn.

'Sometimes students come in and it's just they don't know how far a student with physical disability can move, or sometimes they mother them too much, but as an LSA with performing arts experience I know they can move their bodies a lot more than that. With visually impaired students sometimes part of the role is moving their bodies to show them what to do... so you need to know how bodies move. An LSA who wasn't performing arts trained would move the body in a different way.

'Some students don't have a problem working with an integrated group straight away, but others come in with the teenage attitude, it's normal, of 'it's cool to be with those people but not those people' [physical disability]. When you come in with all of that and then you see the LSA, someone who is a role model type figure, doing a duet with the person in a wheelchair it changes that.

'When I was a student on the BTEC First Steven [Murphy] was the LSA in the group and he was someone I looked at and felt I could aspire to, because of his ability in dance and because of the way he worked with us.

'Students come up to me and ask me advice about dance at the end of classes, or about career options, especially towards the end of the year, many of them have seen me perform [at Stratford Circus, or in a film]'.

Steven Murphy, LSA to the BTEC First group 2002-3

Steven studied at NewVIc between 1992 and 1995, joining the college in its first year. He undertook the BTEC First in performing arts, went on to complete the BTEC National in performing arts and won a place at Laban Centre London to study dance, following strong intervention from the college to secure discretionary local authority support for paying his fees. This was before the DfES Dance and Drama Award Scheme had been established. Having graduated from Laban he established his own dance company and returned to NewVIc to work as a sessional tutor and LSA.

Clare Connor (teacher of dance at NewVIc from 1996-2002) had identified the need for a LSA who had an understanding of the skills and techniques of performing arts, and who would not be afraid to work physically with students and get involved in practical workshop activity. Steven said:

'LSAs at NewVIc themselves are trained in the Performing Arts – in a group with able-bodied and disabled-bodied students it keeps them all moving and working so that when the teacher is with one half of the group I can be with another, and having another opinion on the dance work in class helps the teacher. It's different working as an LSA in Performing Arts because it's all about how the group works together. They will get marked on working with others, and it's about how the other students work with the disabled students. In other subjects it's totally different as I will only be working with the disabled student, or the teacher, it isn't about the whole group adapting. And because in the art medium you can make choices on the final piece to some extent to allow the adaptation of the group.' (interview, 2003)

One year on

What did the students remember the most about the BTEC First course a year later? We followed up the end of study interviews with further discussion in spring 2004. Without hesitation, it was performing in Stratford Circus that had stuck in their memories 'because of performing to a live audience'. This was because of the buzz of performing on stage and how the piece had allowed the group to function well together, affirming a sense of achievement, applied skills, and mutual support.

Jon: 'I want to do auditions now, don't mind at all, I didn't feel like that before. It's because of the rush of finishing the show, like the dance show we did, at the end it's the best feeling.'

The language of the students in conversation with Rachel a year on showed that they recognised that creativity was an important skill to have developed.

Sonya: 'I use my imagination more this year, I give my ideas to the group more. It's because I know more, I know I have the skills this year. We just did monologues in drama, and you've got to be creative to do the monologues, to get the ideas for it in time, you've got to be creative with language to do monologue'

Abdul: 'I'm used to working with professionals now. I have developed creatively through doing all the aspects of the course.' Again, the variety of opportunity on offer is an important factor in nurturing creative skills.

Looking back on the BFD, two of the sample group reflected on how they could see it as a preparatory year in building skills:

Abdul: 'this year we know the territory, last year it was more like preparation, now we've got to know the places we're working in and what we're doing, now we're concentrating on our work and what we're doing... this year the group works much better together... everyone is taking it more seriously because they're thinking about the future now'

Sonya: 'we are about to audition for the final piece... I've got a really different feeling about it to last year. These are proper auditions... because it's like what the professionals do, they are treating us more like adults now'

Students were using slightly more technical vocabulary at this stage, and they spoke with more fluency about their art form.

Jessica: 'This year I joined xyz dance group, it's a dance group for ages up to 25, boys and girls, two others from this group are also doing it. When I first started at NewVIc I thought I would join a dance group, but only once I'd got the skills.'

Sonya: 'This year I have joined an after school group for kids as a volunteer once a week... I have used the improvisation games with them that we did last year'

Some conclusions

Students come to see that there is a weaving together of the worlds of formal learning and informal participation in the micro-world of the arts at NewVIc. For example in the music block they see posters which advertise bands performing locally and at Stratford Circus. They have teachers who are active as performers, composers, choreographers and directors in the world outside. Artists and arts companies with which they come into contact (and their LSAs, most of whom are ex-NewVIc students) are more representative than their teachers of the diversity of experiences, aspirations and influences in the group. The arts marketing materials with which they are surrounded show professional artists and companies where they will be performing in a couple of months time. This gives them a sense that they are moving into the same arena as professional performers.

These factors help to build the sense of ownership which we observed these students assume over their work and learning. The ownership built up slowly from half way through the year when they had bonded as a group due to the various team exercises and had a final project which involved them all. At this point, they know they will be seen by a live audience at the year's end and this builds up their concentration.

Students are made aware of additional learning opportunities and local community arts activity. Talented individuals were pushed to take their abilities further afield and to a higher level. For example, Mez, one of the BFD students who became very successful on the course by the end of the year, sang a duet with a fellow student in the mid year music concert and made an impression. He described this as a test to see whether he could sing in front of people, because in school it had been a negative ordeal for him:

> In the school concert I was shaking, the microphone was shaking, I was doing everything wrong like I was looking at the floor, not looking out at the audience, not using my voice properly, I wasn't expressing my feelings in the way I was doing it. I had really wanted to get through to the finals... this time I could do it... [end of year comment] I want to be a performer, the same as what I wanted at the beginning of this course. I know I can be on stage in front of people now.

He and a fellow student, Meena, joined a local gospel choir who perform at community venues around the borough, encouraged by a music teacher who also led the gospel group.

In parallel with the development of flexibility in group interaction, the artist-professionals the students are to be directly involved with are introduced gradually, so that the experience is cumulative. The process of building blocks of experience gradually take the students outside the college and into more professional situations. And they are surrounded by other groups of students going through similar projects and encouraged to work with and learn from them.

Success stories?

There is a sense in which the metanarrative of 'achievement and excellence', the college's marketing strapline, is used by teachers to develop processes for students to experience success. The stories from this research represent a view of student achievement which shows growth and development, and for teachers it becomes important to tell such stories year after year. But student success within these programmes should not be seen simply as a unidirectional upward curve. Developing students' self-confidence as learners, which may or may not equate to success in an academic context, is a fragile process and depends at all times on sensitivity in interpersonal relations.

For some of the students who did not complete the course, external events made continuing at college impossible. Many faced economic or housing problems and were under pressure from their families to bring in income, and to justify their attendance at college in terms of future career prospects. To some extent, the Education Maintenance Allowance (EMA) scheme, providing support for students from families on low incomes to stay in FE and linking this support to attendance, has made a difference. Nonetheless the motivation to continue to attend and participate needs to be intrinsic and reinforced by positive learning experiences. EMA may have had softer impacts in mitigating some of the financial pressure on students, allowing them more time to study, reducing the need for them to work part time and improving attendance, but we do not have statistical data over enough time from NewVIc to prove or disprove this.

The fact that three of our sample of six left the course before the end of the year shows that the script of success does not come easily. Some students commented on the demanding nature of the programme – particularly in the level of commitment required to the group – reliability, punctuality, support for others, and self-reflectiveness. Not all students were able to make such personal commitment to the group, due to their previous experiences, current life-events, and ability to trust teachers or other students.

Equally, success should not be defined as simply passing the course – for some, the experience of sustaining attendance over a year is real progress. Some students were clear by the end of the programme that a career in performing arts was not for them and went on to study in business and health and social care. Clearly the intermediate qualification in performing arts (equivalent to four GCSEs) had built their confidence as learners, helped them to clarify their objectives, and move on. Achievement in this context is multifaceted. The distance travelled and level of skills developed will be different for each person.

The stress on achievement and excellence does risk less attention being paid to negative experiences, or less value being placed upon students who have may have made major achievements in the context of their life stories, in spite of not completing the programme. Simon, for example, 'failed' the programme but nonetheless progressed to a local college to study music.

Undertaking this research has made us more aware of the power dynamics at play in the college setting; teachers' ability to exercise judgement, to reward, to include or exclude. To make learning successful with these young people there is a continual need to maintain a critical and self-reflective orientation, which is emotionally and physically exhausting and which relies upon colleagues and the institutional climate for support. A narrative of success – a belief that students can succeed and that the college can meet their needs – is required so as not to become exhausted. However, this should not prevent staff from analysing the dynamics of inclusion and ex-clusion within the programme. Research processes such as this study, in particular the researcher working in partnership with teachers, may help to uncover and illuminate some of these tensions and conflicts.

4

Home

Jo Parkes

This chapter describes Home, *an additional learning project at NewVIc that ran from 2000-2002, and the research surrounding it. In 2003 the impact of the project on the individuals and organisations involved was evaluated through interviews with them. In 2003-2004, two studies tested the transferability of the* Home *project model and general principles of project work at NewVIc.*

Description of the project

Making the film *Home* brought together ten artists and hundreds of other people from two countries. Three teams of artists – each made up of a choreographer, filmmaker and composer – worked with performers in three locations, East London and Somerset in the UK, and Washington DC in the US, to make dance-based film and video pieces exploring the notion of 'home'. Participants in the London and Taunton films changed places, spending a night in their partner's home to research the theme. Students from all three locations exchanged work by video and email.

At NewVIc, three teacher-artists worked with a cast of twenty-six people aged from 10 to 70. I conceived and choreographed the project and developed the NewVIc film in collaboration with the director, Anton Califano, and composer, Robert Wells. The cast was made up of four students from intermediate to degree level programmes at NewVIc, seven students from four local secondary schools, Langdon, Lister, St Angela's and

Sarah Bonnell, one primary school pupil, the families of three of the students, three community members and two professional dancers. Other students worked on the film as assistants, in choreography and production. The film was produced by Dhiraj Mahey of Primal Pictures and shot over eight days by a professional crew, with trainees from NewVIc, including the industry-centred film school and from local schools. Teacher-artist Angela Diskin worked with BTEC Art and Design students to create costumes for the film. Graphics students at the college created the poster for the film.

The project sought to offer training opportunities to students, as well as allowing them to build relationships with older students and professionals, identifying pathways through education into the dance and film industries. Professionals acted as mentors to students, who in turn mentored less experienced students, transferring skills and modelling behaviour. The rehearsal period extended over six months, to allow relationships to develop. The integration of the students' families into the project sought to strengthen support networks for the students by allowing families to share the process of artistic creation so they would invest in the work and gain understanding of the wider transferable skills developed. The teacher-artists from all three locations came together to lead collaborative work-shops, developing their practice and forming relationships with their peers. In this way, the project sought to offer learning opportunities to everyone taking part.

Some of the cast for the film were recruited through workshops in the four local secondary schools. About sixty students in all were involved. After the student cast had been selected, we auditioned for two professional per-formers. Students improvised with the dancers and had a strong voice in who was cast. The dancers were chosen for their abilities to work with the students as well as for their performance skills.

The creative process began with students from urban east London and rural Taunton spending a night in each other's homes and exploring this ex-perience through dance, sound and video tasks. The cast rehearsed to-gether for four hours every Saturday and in small groups one evening a week for six months.

The NewVIc film premiered alongside the Washington DC video at Stratford Picture House, east London in July 2002. It has since been screened at dance and film festivals in London, Monaco, Barcelona, Hamburg, New York, Buenos Aires and Cologne.[1]

Background

The project is in many ways typical of the learning context of NewVIc. The arts and media team have a long history of implementing project work as an opportunity for situated learning in real-life contexts. There is also a history at the college of vertical learning projects, in which people of different ages and experiences work together to create performance pieces. These projects open up a space in which students are required to engage in dialogue with people unlike themselves, who might challenge their opinions, values, attitudes and behaviour. The teacher becomes co-learner; a member of a group of people investigating an idea, rather than the deliverer of knowledge. She is allowed to be a person, with her own life history, her experience just one of many. Group members model behaviour for each other, articulate experiences and knowledge and pass on learning. Students are required to formulate their own opinions and decide upon their attitudes and behaviour, drawing upon a wider range of experiences than would be possible with a group of peers and one teacher.

Some of the cast had spent most of their lives in east London. Others had travelled many miles from their country of birth, some as refugees in difficult circumstances. In the recruitment of the cast, emphasis was placed upon the performers' engagement with the theme rather than their skills base. The theme of the piece was chosen specifically to invite the cast to engage with their different personal experiences.

As discussed elsewhere in this book, this model of project work relates to Paulo Freire's work on a dialogical approach to learning (Freire, 1998b). This approach sees a teacher not as a person who unloads their knowledge, but as one engaged in an exchange of knowledge with her students. In the *Home* project model, a diverse group of people are exchanging experience and learning. The teacher interacts with the students as persons rather than as role occupants. The group is engaged in a dialogue which allows difficulty, conflict and uncertainty to exist in the framework of reciprocal regard, rather than the teacher requiring the students to subscribe to her views. It is an educational model which foregrounds the person rather than the knowledge. The chosen theme of the project highlighted the personal nature of the learning.

The project draws on a tradition at NewVIc of work which is inter-disciplinary, devised and collaborative. The process for creating the film draws on the practices of community dance in the UK and the US, which evolved out of the shift towards experimental dance forms in the 60s led by the Judson Church Group in the US and the development of 'new dance' in the UK (Benjamin, 2002). In particular, the project *Home* drew upon my practical experience of the artistic practice of Liz Lerman, Celeste Miller, Victoria Marks and Adam Benjamin. The hallmarks of this work are:

- no distinction made between high and low art forms
- striving for high aesthetic values, created by community members
- an inclusive movement vocabulary, which does not rely upon codified techniques and incorporates everyday and popular movement
- emphasis on process
- site-specific work
- intergenerational work
- interdisciplinary work

Another feature of project work at NewVIc is the model of teacher-artists. Teacher-artists work at the college while sustaining active careers in their professions. Some have full-time teaching commitments and create work during weekends, evenings and holidays. Others work part time; still others are released from teaching through alternative funding sources. Some separate their work at the college from their art making. Others seek to incorporate the two. This is a model of working practice which would be familiar for academic practitioners in a higher education (HE) context but less so in the sixth-form or secondary school context.

The artistic team on *Home* were all teacher-artists working at NewVIc. Two of us were full time – Anton Califano and me – and one, Robert Wells, worked three days a week. Anton and I were released from our teaching commitments for several days a week throughout the project, having won funding for it from London Arts, Awards for All and Skillswork. Robert Wells was paid to work on the project on days when he was not teaching.

The conception and delivery of *Home* was located at the intersection of the artistic team's practice as artists and as teachers, and the intersection of the college with the communities it serves. The meeting of these four elements allowed the evolution of the project. The project model suggests that project leaders can be both teacher and artist, and have a foot in both camps. The notion of the teacher-artist varies from more common models of artist in residence or visiting artist (see, among others, Dust, 1999; Animarts, 2003; Fyfe, 2002), in that the artists with whom students work are, in this case, insiders in the college – teachers – often working in collaboration with external artists.

In this project model, the teacher-artist becomes what Howard Gardner (1993) calls 'an example of productive artistry'. The teacher is not teaching the students one way of doing things, but rather modelling the process of learning, struggling with process, problem-solving, not knowing. Thus she acts as an embodiment of standards. The research discussed below indicates that this modelling is a motivating factor for student achievement and that work as both teacher and artist has a positive effect upon staff recruitment, professional development and retention.

This relates to the current debates about the status of teachers as professionals. Bartlett and Burton (2003) have documented the erosion of teacher autonomy through increased centralisation and the introduction of markets in education and managerialism begun in the 1980s and continued under the current government. As teachers lose control of curriculum content, delivery and assessment, so their status as professionals – autonomous, reflective practitioners – is eroded. Bartlett and Burton see standardisation as a force which limits creativity and autonomy.

The teacher-artist model may allow staff opportunities to work in a more creative and autonomous environment, while addressing the needs of the curriculum. Although this approach seeks to work within the quality assurance mechanisms of the college, it does not begin with them. It begins with the student and teacher experience. Middle managers understand the practice and can evaluate it within staff appraisal mechanisms. Alongside this, teacher-artists define their professionalism within standards of industry practice. Regularly engaged with professionals in the field and often presenting work in the field, staff frame their expectations of the work to the standards existing outside the college.

One way that teacher-artists work with the industry is through the NewVIc's commitment to working in partnership with other organisations to create broader learning contexts and to establish the learning in the real world. The *Home* project was developed in partnership with local film production company, Primal Pictures and supported by the local dance development agency, East London Dance. The film was premiered at Stratford Picture House, a venue in which the performers and their families had seen films screened from around the world. The project also demonstrates the team's commitment to multiple learning sites and a curriculum which encourages students to interact with the local context. The film was shot on location around east London and students worked to source, negotiate and manage locations for the shoot. This self-selected learning, on multiple sites, relates to Gardner's (1993) notions of a future school in which much student learning takes place in a vocational environment matched with the student profile of intelligences.

The project illustrates how the formal and informal curriculum of the arts and media team interacts. Although the project took place outside of the core curriculum, the lead staff on the project took opportunities to network the project into the curriculum, regularly using the theme of 'home' and creative ideas from the process in their curriculum teaching, researching while meeting curriculum objectives. For example, a class of students exchanged choreographic work and feedback with students in Washington DC by video and email and the Art and Design team led a printmaking project using objects found in the home. In this way many more students than participated in the final film got to experience some of the process of making it.

Methodology
Strand 1 – Home
Researcher Rachel Fell interviewed participants in the *Home* project in the twelve months following the project. Interviewees included most of the student participants, two community participants, two professional artists, three teachers in the partner secondary schools, one family of a performer, and senior management figures at NewVIc. At screenings of the film in the feeder schools with whom we worked, Rachel Fell documented comments, questions and discussion among students and staff. Graham Jeffery led a discussion group with the three key artists on the project. This data was collected and analysed, triangulated with me, and forms the basis of our findings on the impact of the project presented in this chapter.

Stand 2 – Teacher-artist
In a second strand of the research, we undertook a wider investigation into the role of the teacher-artist at NewVIc. This included interviews with staff on the arts and media team, questionnaires to the team, staff notes on the impact of past projects and several small-scale creative projects by staff members, investigating specific questions. These included individual and group creative sessions for staff and sessions with students. In one of these projects, the Art and Design team spent two days of activities with external facilitators reflecting on their artistic work and their practices as teachers – the Cromer project. The intention was for staff to push the boundaries of their practice beyond the familiar and evaluate the impact of this on future teaching and learning within the curriculum. Staff documented the impact of the Cromer project on their work in the classroom in creative work and

written documents. Rachel Fell observed these sessions and conducted interviews with staff and students after the sessions.

Stand 3 – Transferability

In a third strand of the research, we undertook two transferability studies. From October 2002 to March 2003, I worked with Kate Saunders at Bridgwater College, an FE college in Somerset, to support in the delivery of a project based upon the *Home* model. Anton and I led creative workshops for the staff and students working on the project. Mark Raeburn, director of photography on *Home* and subsequently a teacher-artist at NewVIc, worked as cameraman on the project. The aim of this research was to identify features of the project which were transferable to the Bridgwater context. I held conversations with Kate every two weeks and kept a journal.

From March 2004 to May 2004, the NewVIc team worked with Brockhill Park School in Kent on another transferability study. We supported assistant headteacher Jackie Mortimer and Robert Jarvis, the artist in residence, in devising a small-scale project, which used some of the features of project work at NewVIc. These features were: team-teaching between staff from different disciplines, projects led by staff rather than visiting artists, collaborative work with artists from outside the team, and project work meeting curriculum objectives. Based on explorations of multiple learning styles, three teachers of dance worked with three teachers of maths or English to deliver the learning outcomes of their classes through movement-based activities[2]. The teachers planned and then delivered two classes together, which they then evaluated. Rachel Fell interviewed staff and students before, during and after the project. I kept a journal throughout and Rachel observed sessions. All this data was collated, analysed and triangulated, and informs this chapter.

Evaluation
The impact of the *Home* project upon the participants

Our analysis offers evidence that the *Home* project helped many of the students who took part to gain greater confidence. Six of the seven secondary school students reported feeling more confident. Three of the four secondary school teachers affirmed the positive effect of the project on the students' confidence and self-esteem. A student said:

> Before I did *Home* I was shy around school, I was shy everywhere but then once I got to meet people, once I got used to other people, once I understood their point of view, once I got what they thought about me, I changed completely.

Rehearsal footage reveals that the students developed skills in dance and performance. Several were articulate about their own progress from early rehearsal footage to the final film. Teachers and students told us that the project had impacted upon their subsequent work. Students said that they found performing arts work easier now. Discussing a participant, one secondary school teacher commented:

> I've noticed his practice is a lot better. He's more professional. He's more focused and he understands the processes... His work in drama has more depth to it. He thinks about things a bit more... He evaluates on a much deeper level.

Two students reported difficulty connecting the project work with their curriculum studies. They wanted projects like this to be part of their curriculum, but could not always articulate the relationship between the two.

> ...the experience was so different to the curriculum work here she didn't connect them up... She said she hadn't thought of it as it seemed so different to the GCSE project work. (Secondary school teacher)

There is evidence of aspirations among some of the students changing:

> The film has made me realise that there's more to the future than I thought there was because before I thought: go to school, finish school, go to college, finish college and then start work or something. But then when I did the film, I thought there is more to life than just working and doing all your set work for school. When I looked really hard into it, I realised that there was something that I really want to do. (Student)

Participants talked about observing the dedication of the professionals working on the film, the determination they needed to reach the standard of performance they wanted, their initial disappointment and emerging understanding about how their work had been edited – even when scenes and performers were cut – and the sheer effort involved in making the film. Teachers saw it as important that the students saw the link between their curriculum and the real world.

> It is different to learning on the course... on the film you are doing it rather than just talking about it. It makes the move from being a student to being a professional. It's the difference between hearing about it and participating in it. (Community participant and former NewVIc student)

In the Brockhill Park transferability study, teachers noticed students, who sometimes struggled with the traditional delivery of material engaging with greater motivation. All student groups felt that they would retain the material studied more easily. One teacher observed that his students were remembering more than usual.

Three of the teachers at the secondary schools noted effects on students who had not participated in the project but were inspired by seeing people they knew performing, perhaps surprised that such an accomplished piece had been created locally. The teachers noticed that the aspirations of students increased, including a willingness to participate in further projects.

Evidence suggests that the project had some impact upon the emotional development of some of the students. Three talked about how they had been able to express feelings which they could not express before. William Yule (1998) has written about the positive effects on refugee students of expressing memories and feelings through art. This may counters a tendency not to talk about their feelings at home, for fear of upsetting their parents. We found this to be true in the *Home* research.

> I told [a fellow performer] a lot of things during *Home*, things I hadn't even told my best friend. That's because I trusted him so much. I [was] so happy to let things out of my mind about how I feel because when you keep something inside, it hurts a lot. Then you let it out, it does a lot of good and that's what happened to me during *Home*. (Student)

This speaking out affected the lead artists. We drew closer to the families and social engagements became important for everyone. But we found listening repeatedly to traumatic stories difficult, and sometimes felt concerned about our ability to support the families through the emotions the project was releasing. We would recommend that in future a professional counsellor work alongside the artists and be available for participants and their families.

The project brought families closer together and drew connections between families from different communities.

> As a family, we dealt with issues we had never talked about. I am mixed race and my nan did not like it at first. We had never spoken about it. We were able to talk to each other about personal things and we have got much closer. (Student)

> The cast felt like they know each other. The project built links across different communities. (Mother of student)

The families who became involved in the project articulated how it had helped them to understand what their child was studying. These three families, though, were already highly supportive of their children and engaged in their learning – hence their enthusiasm for joining in. Students whose families were not as supportive did not involve them in the project.

> She is a very motivated student anyway and she has 100 per cent support from her parents... For other students to be involved with something like this would be more difficult if they didn't have that kind of support in place. They need to have that kind of commitment and motivation already there for this kind of project. (Secondary school teacher)

The project was extra curricular and the students who participated in the final film were carefully chosen. It would be difficult to get performances of such quality from students who were not specially selected or were less reliable. This is supported by the findings of both the Bridgwater transferability study and teacher responses about this issue on other projects which worked with small groups of students, rather than whole classes. But we did strive to make the selection process for *Home* as inclusive as possible. We asked teachers not to select the students who had the highest grades or the best technique but those who were keen to take part and most likely to benefit.

The experience of vertical learning
Many students and community performers were enthusiastic about the wide range of ages and experiences and the way people learned from one another.

> It was good learning from each other. I picked up ideas watching other people dance and seeing their thinking. Before I wouldn't have paid much attention to that. (Student)

> I learnt an enormous amount from the [students'] experience, their enthusiasm and acceptance... Part of the special thing is having all ages and backgrounds together. (Community participant)

The more experienced students felt they had learned from mentoring younger students but that this work was sometimes insufficiently acknowledged. Students learned from the professional dancers by mastering specific skills, observing their commitment and professional behaviour on the long cold days of shooting, and the informal conversations they had about progression routes through the industry. Many of the professionals who worked on the project enjoyed their engagement with the students. They believed their relationship with them was less formal than the teacher-artists on the project.

One of the performers asked for more guidance on how to interact with the students. While the lead teacher-artists sought to support the professionals in their engagement with the students, more formal briefing or training might be appropriate in similar projects.

Progression routes appeared to be created at all levels, from primary school pupils through to community participants and professionals. At least eight of the performers have since worked on other projects, both with the partners on Home and independently. One of the secondary school students is now excelling on the BTEC National course at NewVIc. He did not get the required grades at GCSE to enter the course but achieved direct entry because of his prior learning and the commitment he had demonstrated through the project. Currently he has the strongest grade profile of his group and is a role model for his peers. One HND student who supported the costume design has since been employed at NewVIc, as have four of the industry professionals who volunteered their time to work on the film. Several of the student participants now work as assistants or leaders on similar projects, and the professional trainees moved on into further employment or training in the film industry.

The formal and informal curriculum

A host of informal learning opportunities emerge around a project like Home.

> Put a media student on a professional film set for a day and they will suddenly understand so much more about making films than they would in a year of watching films in a classroom, talking about it, or making their own videos. (Anton Califano, director)

The context of NewVIc means that students may lack the skills to negotiate observing or apprenticeship opportunities for themselves. If the projects are based in the college and led by their teachers, students have the confidence to work on them because enough of the context is familiar. We found that after such experiences students can more easily progress to working outside the college. And students who did not work directly on the project also witnessed the working practices of professionals.

> A lot of the second years saw me coming into the edit suites when we were editing. They saw the sheer amount of work that it took; they began to see how the whole thing was pieced together; they saw rough cuts as we were doing it. (Anton Califano, director)

The form and content of the film was seen to influence dance and video students, who are now choosing controversial themes and more experimental forms for their work. HND students who studied the film articulated how its subject matter and form had inspired them.

If the project were embedded in the formal curriculum, assessment would become more important. We did not track individual learning, which was perhaps a weakness. At NewVIc, the personal tutor plays a key role in assessment, helping the student to identify areas of their experience inside and outside the college for which they can claim outcomes, and helping to identify and track the achievement of personal goals. A flexible, open curriculum, such as that provided by the BTEC qualification framework, helps staff to develop more extended models of vocational learning. In the Brockhill Park transferability study, teachers expressed anxiety about needing to 'get through' the curriculum and prepare their students for exams that assess learning in prescribed ways. A sense of losing time to project work caused some of the teachers stress.

Teacher as learner

> I think I would have forgotten the film if it was not related to me or the local area in some way. It is something that my tutor has made. I can refer to it and ask questions about it. It's something that we are more likely to enjoy because we have a relationship to the teacher. It makes me think 'I can do that'. (HND year 2 student who did not work on the film)

Even if not directly involved in the project or the curriculum-based research phases, the students recognise some of the performers in the film, they know the artists who worked on the film and recognise the locations, so their engagement with it as a teaching resource is heightened.

Students observed their teachers being engaged in a creative process. They saw what long hours the team worked; they witnessed creative conflicts, problem-solving and how much commitment it took to complete the film. The teacher-artists showed them rough cuts of the film and asked for feedback. Students saw their teachers working alongside them on the same equipment as they use, facing challenges similar to theirs.

> They (the teachers) have not just written papers, they have actually done it. It's confidence building. I think: 'If Jo can do it, I can do it' (HND year 2 student who did not work on the film)

> You feel the teachers are learning with you. They do not pretend to know it all. They took risks and some of their ideas did not work. They were prepared to fail. (HND year 2 student who did not work on the film)

Before the delivery of the project, four out of six teachers involved in the Brockhill Park transferability study said they were worried about maintaining discipline while in a learning situation alongside their students. They were reassured to find that they had managed to maintain discipline while demonstrating their ability to learn with the students in a non-traditional learning environment. Interestingly, most students thought that because there were two teachers in each class, they had more control, not less.

Impact of the project on teacher-artists

As Mark Pearson's artwork (above) demonstrates, the impact of approaches of this kind upon teacher-artists is complex. 'Creativity', 'opportunity' and 'freedom' sit alongside 'time' and 'I could be in my studio'.

NewVIc has an imaginative interpretation of its mission and a willingness to learn and share – not least because of the need to develop new learning strategies in what can be a challenging working environment. This context opened up a space in which we could develop the *Home* project. The fact that the team had worked together and collaborated on smaller projects gave a foundation for a more ambitious project. Working in the same building facilitated discussions and development of the film.

As emerging artists, the project gave Anton, Robert and me the opportunity to work on a scale unavailable to us outside the educational setting. The resources of the college and its partner organisations greatly extended the cash budget of the film.

Discussions with the teacher-artists working on this and other projects indicate that such work allows them opportunities for professional development, encouraging them to remain at the college. Released from narrow definitions of what it is to be a teacher, the teacher-artists can re-define their role project by project, thus sustaining professional motivation and enabling career progression outside the established route. The impact upon their professional standing and self-esteem is marked. In a survey of the arts and media team, the three factors most likely to maintain motivation as a teacher were teamwork, a mentally stimulating and challenging role and having a creative role.

The teacher-artists from *Home* are also clear about the impact of project work on their work in the core curriculum.

> It has impacted massively on my teaching. There is a big difference between teaching about using something and using something yourself... I have learned different techniques I had never come across before, which I have now taken into my teaching. (Robert Wells, composer)

> I could probably say that every day something happens which is directly or indirectly related to the film. (Anton Califano, director)

Staff members on other projects record a similar expansion of skills and techniques in their art forms and renewed confidence in their ability as practitioners. Students report that staff become more enthusiatic and motivated and bring new techniques and approaches to classes. This was particularly marked in the responses of art and design students after the Cromer project and evident also in the Brockhill transferability study in which students identified new ideas and a more relaxed approach from their teachers as key factors in collaborative delivery. Three weeks after the end of the project three out of six Brockhill teachers had incorporated elements from the project into their everyday classroom delivery. All the teachers reported having learned from team-teaching, and particularly from observing different teaching styles.

Aside from the benefits to the staff and curriculum development at NewVIc, our analysis suggests that the staff in the feeder schools also benefited. The theme and content of the piece moved some of the teachers and made them think about their students' lives.

It brought home to me that students arrive from different experiences. When a refugee student arrives all you see is a sheet of paper with written details of their past, you don't actually know anything of what this means. It made me think differently about where people come from and join the school from and a general awareness about students (Secondary school teacher)

Staff discussed how observing the process of the film had influenced their curriculum development and alerted them to skills they themselves wanted to develop. The process helped them to see the capabilities of the students working on the project, challenging what they saw as their tendency to underestimate them. This tendency was also evident in the Brockhill Park transferability study, in which four out of six teachers said they revised their assessment of the capabilities of certain students' abilities after seeing them work with a different teacher or in a new context.

Advantages of the role of teacher-artist

Insider knowledge allowed staff constant access to resources which a visiting artist could not easily tap. We had keys to resource rooms, knew which rules which could be bent in times of need and had relationships with site and management staff when we needed special dispensation.

We could also spot opportunities to source funding, both in cash and in kind, thanks to working in an environment where curriculum and budgetary decisions are made collectively. The team had established relationships with the finance and management team and so we could create flexibility within college systems. We set up a separate bank account to manage the budget so that decisions could be quickly made.

The role of middle management in the evolution of project work was important. Middle managers were vital negotiators between the needs of the project and the systems of the college. Their positive, can-do approach facilitated the launch of the project. Without their agreement, support in developing the ideas, fundraising, resolving conflicts, and a willingness to go the extra mile, the project would never have happened. As junior staff, we felt supported by the middle management team and trusted them to work with the accountability systems of the college to convey the nature of our work.

Our experience as teachers helped us deliver the project. Over the six-month rehearsal period, we drew on classroom experience, in particular in working with, and motivating, students from Newham. This was something the visiting artists who were less familiar with an inner-city context sometimes found challenging.

We also understood the needs of our fellow teachers in the partner schools. Teachers welcomed having the project team write letters to parents, type schedules and do the calling and chasing of students and not having to do it themselves. When projects are led by artists who have no experience as teachers, the teacher can sometimes end up in the role of project manager/administrator, preventing them from fully engaging in the creative process.

While students gain by experiencing their teachers as artists, they also benefit from having external industry professionals working with them. Relationships are less formal and allow students access to a wider range of experience. As Hamish Fyfe (2002) among others has noted, artists may have higher expectation of students than their teachers do, because they don't know them, tending towards perfectionism in their own work. They may have more energy because they are not worn down by the daily responsibilities teachers have to shoulder.

> I noticed they were responding well to professional artists – better than with their teachers here. They were more willing to go with it and try new things. If it was me teaching them they would be more resistant to something different and just look at me in a funny way. (Secondary school teacher)

Problems with being a teacher-artist

My relationship with the project participants was different from my relationship with my students when I working in the core curriculum. As a teacher, I place the needs of my students at the centre of my work. When I am involved in a creative process with them, I essentially see my role as facilitating their learning and development. In this project, I had an equal – or stronger – commitment to creating a strong piece of work which reflected my aspirations as an artist.

So I would barely explain the reasons for my decisions. I gave people fewer opportunities to have a part in the process of cutting the film, so that I could focus on the product. Anton and I made editing decisions which left the performances of some of the participants on the cutting-room floor. The needs of the participants at times came second to the agenda of making the best possible film.

So could a project of this kind exist within the mainstream provision at the college, when the core aim is to facilitate learning for all students at all levels? Mapping the work into the core curriculum in the research and development phase and using the film as a teaching resource are attempts to address this. But the core funding for staff time on the film came from external sources – from London Arts and Awards for All.

For the teacher-artists sustaining the balance between the demands of the project and the demands of the core curriculum was difficult, particularly when the project or the curriculum came under pressure. The project was created on site, using many NewVIc resources, so it was impossible to have discrete time when the team were working as artists or could shelve our responsibilities as teachers. The split focus between teaching and artistic activity made it difficult to immerse ourselves wholly in a creative process.

The three lead artists on *Home* have all stated that they would not want to take on a similar project again in such circumstances. It simply required too much from us in terms of time and energy, while we struggled to balance the other responsibilities of our jobs.

The findings of the transferability study support our own. Kate Saunders, the project manager and lead teacher at Bridgwater College had not realised how much work was involved in doing such a project and was clear that she would only give so much time again if she had her workload reduced proportionally. The staff at Brockhill Park kept stressing how difficult it is to balance project work with the demands of the core curriculum and the duties of teachers. The biggest inhibiting factor in taking on project work was the lack of time. This was particularly evident in the secondary schools.

It seems that without altering staff's job descriptions and timetables, such projects are only possible if individuals are prepared to take on an excessive workload and the concomitant stress. Often the people willing to do this are the younger teacher-artists who have more energy and stand to gain most from the opportunities. This raises questions about the sustainability and wider applicability of such projects.

The transferability studies revealed that teachers were more likely to engage with a project if they had chosen to do so, rather than having it was imposed upon them. As Jacqui Mace, a former senior manager at NewVIc, put it: 'Where it works it's because the idea of the project comes from the staff themselves.'

Two years after the completion of the project, both Anton and I are now part-time employees of the college and have shifted much of our project work into a more traditional freelance model.

The process of creating the film
There are questions about the ownership of the stories in the film. The process of sourcing the movement and stories of the film was collaborative.

The performers responded to creative tasks and movement material and stories from family history were brought to light. The cast themselves selected the stories to be told and participated in the development of the telling of these stories. Family members chose to join the process of the piece however they wanted to. Some came to rehearsals; others met us regularly in their homes, before finally talking on camera. Once the film had been shot, however, decisions on editing the footage were made entirely by the artistic team, although the families were shown the fine cut of the film and given the opportunity to respond to the film. At the request of one family, several shots were removed.

This is a model of artistic practice in which the artist engages in dialogue with a community, and undertakes a form of 'portrait-painting'.[3] The film was always intended to be documentary so the artistic choices of the choreographer, director and composer framed the stories of the participants.

Michael Fielding (1999a) discusses the notion of 'authorship' over material, as opposed to 'ownership'. While the language of ownership is often used to represent a positive experience, Fielding believes it can be an exercise in removing power from students, forcing acceptance of a teacher's ideas to such a degree that the ideas become theirs by commitment. Authorship, on the other hand, '...brooks no deceit; you are either involved in the process of exploration and articulation of meaning which authorship involves, or you are not' (Fielding, 1999a, p81).

Undeniably, once the process of structuring the material generated by the cast began, the participant experience shifted away from this notion of authorship, reducing the educational potential of the project. This raises questions around the notion of representation. How should one respond to the ethical dilemmas involved in telling other peoples' stories, and representing them?

David Trend (1997) discusses the tendency of artists to move into education, appropriating difference for our own ends – to access stories, to accumulate more resources. The outsider can offer an alternative perspective, but this perspective may be based upon a superficial engagement with the community, what Trend describes as 'the unfortunate tendency of many artists to assume they can make short-term forays into new social contexts without making long-term commitments to understanding or working in those contexts' (Trend, 1997, p255).

I felt that I belonged to the community whose stories I was exploring. I had been working full-time at the college for two years when I conceived the project and the idea for the piece had evolved through conversations with my students, many of whom had recently arrived in England. The story was also, in a sense, mine – I too had lived a long way from home and struggled with how to establish a sense of rootedness. I made this explicit to the cast; as the participants explored their stories, I explored and shared mine. I sought to make the process as inclusive as possible.

In *The Lure of the Local*, Lucy Lippard (1997) argues for an updated 'regionalism' in art, to counter globalisation and commodification. She discusses art which is rooted in its local context, while being critical and reflective of that context and its relationship to the larger picture. She calls this 'art of place' as opposed to 'art about place'. Community arts practitioners should have as their goal the cultivation of local artistic voices. Lippard suggests that as a form of radical education public art could be used to fulfil a learning component of high school curricula.

The project *Home* might be seen as an example of 'art of place'. The teacher-artists leading the project fit Lippard's definition of belonging to a community through sustained commitment and engagement with that community. The performers were offered pathways onto further projects, courses and access to resources which would enable them to develop their own artistic work. Thus art is created from those within the learning community, rather than people who come from outside. Several participants are now studying or creating work at NewVIc and its partner organisations. In Richard Owen Geer's words, the art made is 'of, by and for' that community (Geer, 1993, p28).

Lippard suggests that the evolution of 'art of place' will require funding agencies to take risks on local emerging artists and be committed to long-term project models. The *Home* project model offers a way in which teacher-artists and students can undertake large-scale, long-term projects which address social and educational agendas. The college becomes a site for creative enterprise.

The professional status of teachers
The project caused debate about the relationship between the artistic output of individuals as opposed to their role as full time employees of the college. This has been manifested in arduous negotiations about the intellectual property rights to the film. Ultimately the college agreed to a four way split in the intellectual property rights to the film between the college,

the production company Primal Pictures, Anton Califano and me. Anton and I were concerned that the college recognise that the commitment, work and skills it took to produce the film were way beyond anything reflected in our job descriptions. The college wanted to have its key role in the development of the project recognised, to protect its considerable financial investment and to frame the project within its public role as a site for shared creative processes between artists, teachers and the community.

This way of working can bring teachers into conflict with the parameters which define their work. It pushes at the boundary of teacher identity: the teacher is artist, researcher, even activist (see Chapter 5). NewVIc exists on the margins of the HE culture, where teachers are expected to engage in individualised research, and FE, where a research culture is barely present. This evolvement of this liminal place allows projects such as *Home*, which exist on the boundaries of teaching, research and community engagement. These projects push at the boundaries of a sixth form college teacher's job and can become the site of – occasionally creative – conflict.

Working in partnership

The *Home* project demonstrates both the advantages and difficulties of working in partnership. Certainly the evolving network of organisations working on the film allowed the project to expand massively. But the management of such partnerships is complex and time-consuming. Very little project management support was built into the project; essentially Anton, Robert and I were project managing in our free time. I had little experience of managing projects of this scale. And we all had fairly heavy teaching timetables, so were seldom accessible by telephone during working hours. So management of the partnerships was not always ideal. This was evident from the failure to complete the Taunton video, or to get the Taunton students to the premiere, the delayed screenings in the partner schools and complicated relationships with the production company. Any similar project would have to have better support for project management.

Conclusion

The research demonstrates that the participants, project leaders and the college community gained a good deal from the project. Reactions to the film indicate that it powerfully communicates stories of a kind seldom heard. Staff and students at NewVIc and in the surrounding schools respond with enthusiasm to the film as a teaching resource and it has acted as a motivating factor in the development of subsequent projects.

Home offers a project model in which students and teacher-artists can work in an open-ended learning situation that foregrounds collaboration and investigation. This establishes a more dialogical relationship between teacher and student, enhancing both student achievement and staff motivation. The research highlights issues surrounding the sustainability of such projects in relation to the workload and roles of teacher-artists, the intense resource demands and the relationship of such projects to what the college defines as its core work. All this has implications for the transferability of the project model to other contexts.

Notes

1   For a detailed explanation of the project, a documentary film about the process, and resources to support teachers and students in studying the film and delivering a similar project, see Parkes and Califano, 2004.

2   This work was based upon a project model developed by Celeste Miller as part of the community dance programme of the Jacob's Pillow Dance Festival in Massachusetts, on which I worked in 2001. Drawing upon Gardner's work on multiple intelligences, the project seeks to deliver the school curriculum in a way which might address the needs of kinaesthetic learners. Each year dance artists work in a high school for two fortnight-long blocks of time, collaborating with teachers to deliver their curriculum, be it maths, biology, pottery etc, through dance and physical activities.

3   I am indebted to my many conversations with Victoria Marks for this idea, which she developed in reference to her own work. She discusses the notion in the programme note to her piece, *Sites Pacific*, performed at the opening of the Getty Center in Los Angeles in 1998.

5

Professional identities:
artist and activist teachers?

Graham Jeffery

What are the implications of the case studies for teacher practice and artistic practice? This chapter explores how the ways of working set out in the case studies affected teachers' professional identities and aspirations. It proposes an expanded model of the teacher as artist/cultural intermediary/social entrepreneur, in light of the weave of personal and professional development for teachers who work at NewVIc.

Teacher-artist identities

Lawrence Stenhouse (1986) threw down a gauntlet in his essay 'Curriculum research, artistry and teaching'. In developing a theory of teacher professionalism based on a subtle and thoughtful analysis of the artistry and the craft of teaching, he opened up a seam of enquiry about the relationship of personal identity, the application of creative skills, relationship-building with learners and reflective practice. He defines the word art as 'a skill expressive of meaning' (1986, p105).

> Teaching is the art which expresses in a form accessible to learners an understanding of the nature of that which is to be learned... The construction of a personal perception of our world from the knowledge and traditions that our culture makes available to use is a task that faces not only the teacher, but also the student, and teaching rests on both partners in the process being at different stages in the enterprise. This is clear to us when we watch a great musician teaching a master class, but it tends to be obscured

in schools in the ordinary classroom... Good learning is about making, not mere doing. (Stenhouse, 1986, p106)

To be an effective teacher, one must have endless curiosity for learning, and be willing constantly to interrogate and play with the impact of one's practice, adjust and make changes, in order to improve learning. He writes:

All good art is an enquiry and an experiment. It is by virtue of being an artist that the teacher is a researcher... the way ahead is to disseminate the idea of teacher as artist with the implication that artists exercise autonomy of judgement founded upon research directed towards the improvement of their art. (Stenhouse, 1986, p107)

This generalised notion of the teaching process as involving artistry, skill, craft and creativity is appealing to practitioners who wish to define themselves as creative individuals and who prioritise creative processes in their work in the classroom. It has appeal as a counter to the 'loss of autonomy' Jo Parkes refers to in Chapter 4; without artistry, the argument goes, the teacher is reduced to a functionary, a bureaucrat or a quality assured trainer. But as Jo implicitly acknowledges, there are two related questions that need to be unravelled if the notion of teacher-artist is to have currency:

■ In whose interest is the artistry of the teacher? For Stenhouse, the art of teaching means that the learning needs of students form the basis for the teacher's enquiry. In Jo Parkes' model of teacher-artist practice, teacher and student are engaged in a shared artistic enquiry led by the teacher-artist, which is driven more by the content and questions set by the project than by any pre-determined curriculum. This is a risky way of working, since teacher creativity and artistic creativity in this model exist in an ambivalent relationship to the prescribed curriculum. Nonetheless the learning model, as the research shows, is rich and strongly impacts on student aspirations and understandings. So do we need an ethics of teacher-artist practice that is framed within an overall ethics of teacher professionalism?

■ On what principles should the educating partnership between teacher and artist be based? The role of teacher and the visiting artist differ. This is generally because one is a permanent member of staff, the other a visitor. Each brings different perspectives to the educating process – which makes this dialogue extremely valuable.

In 2001, a consortium named Animarts, led by LIFT and the Guildhall School of Music and Drama, undertook an action-research study exploring the conditions for effectiveness in partnership between teachers and artists. The Animarts report, *The Art of the Animateur* (2003) argued for the relationship between artists and teachers to be built upon equality and mutual reflection. Enough time for serious planning and evaluation between the parties was identified as essential for successful partnership. The report suggested that there must be acknowledgement that the creativity in the partnership is shared, likewise the design of the learning process and the responsibility for the learning.

Stenhouse's contention that the skilled professional teacher ought to be thought of as a kind of artist – someone continually exploring, refining, reviewing and developing their practice with learners – helps us reconceptualise the professional identity required if the model of teacher-artist is to have wider currency.

If the teacher is already an artist, why might she need to work with professional artists? Most teachers today would be unlikely to characterise their daily work as that of an artist, so creative partnership might be a way of revitalising their practice. But no one should assume that the creativity in the partnership will be supplied entirely by the artist; and the teaching supplied by the teacher. Muschamp (in Cowling, 2004), drawing on a 1999 Ofsted report, identifies a number of roles for artists in schools: as ' maker and presenter of art, as teacher, as teaching resource, motivator, role-model, outsider and broker...' He goes on to suggest that there may be

> ...possible tensions when artists seem to be intolerant and uninformed about teachers' priorities, or where teachers, who themselves may be highly competent artists, feel uneasy or even threatened by the introduction of another artist into the school. They can also occur when teachers and artists have a different understanding of the intentions of a project... (2004, p37)

The effort to achieve mutual understanding and co-operative ways of working must underpin the process. The weaving together of the conversation between the teacher and artist into learning experiences for students is the basis for partnership.

The model of single teacher – single artist theorised through the discussion and action-research projects which informed in the Animarts report – and work by Woolf and Griffiths (2004) exploring how a model of 'apprenticeship' is relevant to artist-teacher-student relationships – is an abstraction. It is a simplified model of a complex concept which has many overlapping and sometimes contradictory models of dialogue between learners, teachers and artistic practitioners. These range from short residencies, to touring theatre in education or orchestral workshops, to curriculum based enquiry in which arts processes are used to explore other curricular topics., sometimes described as 'arts integration'. There are also extended projects which aim to develop entrepreneurship and business skills or engage young people in community regeneration.

I use the terms teacher and artist to symbolise the different professional roles in a creative partnership between them, as a means to differentiate the institutional role of teacher as professional educator, and the role of creative practitioner, the maker of art, in their engagement with different educational contexts. 'Artist' is one of the most complicated occupational descriptors in the English language. In this chapter I focus on the emerging field of interacting professional roles between teachers and the visiting or resident artist – what in some branches of performing arts have been described as animateurs.

There are four dimensions to the tentative model of creative partnership I propose :

1 the teacher as artist
the creative practice of the teacher, which has an personal and an institutional dimension: an inner conflict in the formation of teacher identity that, skilfully channelled, can be highly creative: this inner conflict and dialogue can be characterised as play, deviance, bending the rules, engaging in dialogue with learners

2 the artist as educator
the artist's role on the boundary between institutional learning and less formal, perhaps more real and situated learning, bringing a portfolio of knowledge, ideas, technical skills and abilities which are complementary to those of the teacher

3 the artistry of teaching
pedagogy: fuelled by the cycle of research-planning-action-reflection theorised in the notion of reflective practice[1]: the methodology for communicating and sharing processes

4 artistic work as a model and educator
the skilled facilitation of participation in creative process – the work of making art[2] – and the value of creative products – works of art – as exemplars, models, resources, and tools for exploration and questions

The teacher as artist

Educators have to deal with tensions about their role as practitioners. Effective teaching requires attention to the art and craft of observation, communication, listening and prompting (see Brice Heath and Wolf (2004a) on visual learning in the primary school). It requires modelling the skills and attributes of the two professions – that of the teacher and that of the field to be taught. A teacher plays multiple roles simultaneously – including but not limited to being a model practitioner, coach, tutor, and representative of the institution.

In the context of vocational learning, the teacher ought to also be a practitioner of what she teaches. This modelling of artistic processes by teachers is a powerful tool for developing student engagement.

The artist as educator

The role of the artist in learning has been extensively explored (see for example Brice Heath and Wolf, 2004a; Woolf, 1999; Dust and Sharp, 1999). The artist in education is frequently an outsider who comes into an educational space and acts as a catalyst or challenger of learning, and who provides ways of exploring the world which involve more sensory, immersive and physically rooted ways of working than are customary in classroom settings. The visiting artist is precisely *not* the teacher – she is the figure of the 'other' who is permitted, within ethical limits, to open new contexts and new frontiers for learning and to present the challenge of the unfamiliar. She brings valuable skills in her areas of practice to the learning setting – inspiring and encouraging learners to develop these skills themselves. Bob Jeffrey (2004), writing for the comparative Creative Learning and Student Perspectives project about the roles of artists in partnership, notes that the artist creates opportunities

> ...to bring to the surface learners' knowledge in a collaborative exercise between artists and learners... working with artists not only brings new perspectives or interests, it also helps support a common theme between teachers and artists, the value of uncovering, sharing, exploring experience. (2004, p2)

The artist helps students to explore the world in new ways. These might be tactile and sensuous, using sound, movement, space, found objects, visual clues, and investigating environments. The artist allows the development of physical skills in handling materials and responding to the world using multiple languages, visual, aural, physical. Because such investigative processes are often based on students' direct experiences, they may strengthen 'the construction of learners as people and weaken the pupilisation of learners' (Jeffrey, 2004, p4).

The artist can play different roles in this process:

- artist as *agent provocateur* in the context of the institution – as questioner and challenger to established practices and procedures

- artist in residence – as artist-practitioner who engages with the college context to generate work with students and individually

- artist as professional model to whom students are apprenticed

- artist as professional engaged in a shared enterprise with students

The skills-sharing undertaken by artists in residence is frequently reported by teachers to give a powerful boost to their own professional development, particularly when the design of the artist's role within the college has been collaboratively conceived and the practices and processes of learning have been shared (see Craft *et al*, 2001; Jeffrey, 2004; Animarts, 2003). Woolf and Griffiths (2004) make the case for an apprenticeship model of creative partnership in which 'interaction with a creative practitioner offers a 'scaffolded' approach to teaching and learning, which enables the learner to find out about, and eventually enter the community of practice of the other practitioners: artist/creative or teacher' (2004, p15).

The artistry of teaching

Beyond Stenhouse's general teaching artistry where the teacher is a creative investigator of learning, the presence of the artist-practitioner-professional in the learning institution allows an appeal to authenticity of experience. Our case studies explore how experiential learning involves students and teachers and artists investigating ideas, processes, and environments together. Skilled dialogue between teachers, artists and arts organisations, within and beyond their immediate communities, opens up new contexts for learning that appeal to students and the community because of their situated character. The model of the teacher-artist depends upon an acceptance of permeable boundaries between an individual's established institutional roles and her interests as a practitioner of the arts. Models in use vary. This teacher may be on his own, developing pedagogical practices which are self-challenging and risk-taking (see Craft, in press, Chapter 5); the teacher and the artist may work in dialogue (see Animarts, 2003), or the work may be on a large scale, involving multidisciplinary teams from a variety of organisational and community contexts (as described in Chapter 4).

A further consequence of this approach is that the learning practices of the artist may come to inform everyday classroom practice more and more: how the artist learns, how the artist investigates and makes material, and how ideas are refined and developed in the creation of artistic products. Such processes have been examined as part of the RESCEN project based at Middlesex University, London. Brice Heath and Wolf (2004b, p8) explore the 'duo of deliberation and accident' involved in the creation of artistic works, and observe that 'the best works of the imagination require intention and invention.' There is a material and environmental dimension to this too. By encountering the working practices of professional artists, while developing the flexibility and openness required for imaginative thought, students may learn technique and skill in manipulating materials. And the presence of professionals may encourage the practical and self-disciplined preparatory skills of, for example, tuning instruments precisely, warming up before a dance class, or carefully maintaining printmaking equipment to become incorporated into the everyday routines of the learners in the arts[3]. The learners become more autonomous practitioners as a consequence of the modelling of practical and conceptual art-making by teachers, artists and peers with whom they are surrounded.

Artistic work as a model and educator

This leads onto the fourth perspective within my tentative model of creative partnership. Better documented and researched than the others, it concerns the value of artistic work and the work of art as a springboard for learning (Eisner, 1972, 1990; Bosch, 1998). Teachers of arts subjects in secondary and further education are required to have professional qualifications and professional experience in the arts, to form the basis for their classroom practice.

Much existing work in arts education literature focuses on this perspective – in particular upon the transmission of cultural traditions, practices, and techniques and the resultant learning (see, for example, Paynter, 1992; Ross, 2003). Much classroom-based arts teaching that has no partnerships takes place in the interaction between perspective 1 and perspective 4.

What makes a creative partnership?

An effective creative partnership needs to deploy all four of these perspectives. It needs to explore and debate the contexts of these four roles – in particular perspective 4 – by investigating and using places and spaces for learning outside of the everyday, and beyond the physical boundaries of the institution, by means of research and investigation. Creative colleges could be crucibles of public, shared and collaborative arts activity. They can become extended, networked institutions along the lines proposed for community music centres (see Everitt, 1997).

Taking the work into a shared public realm, for example incorporating students' work into professional performance spaces as we have done with Stratford Circus, or allowing them to work for extended periods with professionals, situates the work more broadly and allows learners to share their achievements in a public context. And we saw in Chapter 4, it allows a direct connection to be made between the quality standards of professional work and the quality standards at work in the college curriculum. Assessment – at least informally – becomes more than a private dialogue between teacher and student as it is opened to wider scrutiny. Even Swanwick (1999), a strong advocate of a national curriculum for music, points out that unless the barriers are deliberately broken down between musical activity within the formal curriculum and musical work undertaken in community and professional settings, a dangerous polarisation, stagnation and institutionalisation of musical life will result:

> One effect of the drift towards centralised school curricula... is that teaching tends to take place almost entirely in school classrooms. Certainly teacher trainees in the UK and elsewhere are constrained to spend most of their time 'on school premises' and that is where teachers are inspected and expected to be at work... Yet there is a musical richness beyond individual school gates if only we could more systematically find and utilise it. (Swanwick, 1999, p108)

If developed within a broader framework of creative partnership with professional artists, the concept of teacher-artist may enable a dialogical form of education where the assumptions of learners and teachers are challenged and stretched by outsiders. It creates a dynamic in which the idea of cultural production as a locus of identity formation for students and teachers is placed at the heart of the learning institution, but as a negotiated rather than prescribed space.

In a genuinely creative partnership this dialogue operates at multiple levels: it takes place *internally*, as a teacher reflects on her practice; *between colleagues* as they build collaborations; *between teacher and students*; and between a *teacher and the visiting artist(s)*. The idea of crossing boundaries and recombining artistic materials, as the Animarts findings show, provide a further catalyst for creativity:

> Where artists from one art form work on common themes with artists in another art-form (cross-arts) fundamental re-thinking can take place with

new perceptions being gained which affect individual artistic practice. (2003, p65)

Most professional art-forms that have any currency in the marketplace also represent a form of interdisciplinary and intensely collaborative practice, subject to complex chains of production, marketing and reception. Theatre, choreography, film, multimedia, opera, radio and television all rely on complex and multi-level teams, drawing on diverse skill-sets at all stages from conception to realisation. Projects constructed at NewVIc tend to build students' understanding of how to work in multi-disciplinary teams by bringing together groups and teachers from different areas of the curriculum to work on common goals.

NewVIc provides some mechanisms for teams to operate in these multiple roles of teacher-practitioner-artist. Two key identities come into play: the identity of the individual creative practitioner and the professional-institutional identity of the teacher. Etienne Wenger, writing about learning theories based upon notions of communities of practice, suggests:

> Teachers need to 'represent' their communities of practice in educational settings. This type of lived authenticity brings into the subject matter the concerns, sense of purpose... and emotion of participation... Being an active practitioner with an authentic form of participation might be one of the most deeply essential requirements for teaching. (1998, p276-277)

Acknowledging creative tensions

The liminal and intermediary role of the creative teacher cannot be over-emphasised. Creative teachers mediate between the institution and the individual, between the formal and the informal, between private artistic work and public sharing. They often challenge established institutional and professional norms, whilst maintaining an expert perspective as lead learner and working to identified professional ethics. This requires individual willingness and the organisational capacity to risk experimentation and explore new approaches (see Ofsted, 2003b).

Adaptability and a willingness to negotiate with power relations in the classroom and beyond are essential. The questioning of common sense assumptions about what works, and the insistence on the value of that enquiry, are what energise the creative educator.

The creative teacher of the arts – as professional and as artist-activist – can be characterised as ambivalent and full of inner conflict. Given the right conditions, this ambivalence allows a sense of authenticity and genuine engagement to emerge. Carol Becker, writing about her role in 'crossing worlds and living on the borders of several disciplines' as artist, educator, writer and administrator, observes that artists

> ...also identify with the exile, the one who is spiritually, if not literally, removed from his or her land – and is neither assimilated or assimilable... It is finally the refusal of the artist to fit in, to conform to this regimentation, that makes the image of the artist so powerful within the culture. The artist is the living negation of the society: at the same time, he or she is the best representer of the society. (Becker, 1997, p22)

Not all artists would recognise this definition as applying to them. But developing projects within which teachers explore their positions on the boundary between institutions and communities, between individual learners and qualifications bureaucracies, between art-making and critical judgment, as both institutional insider and creative outsider, provides a place where transformative experiences might be activated. Conversations and collaboration between educators, artists and cultural workers and institutions provide spaces where this kind of engagement might flourish[4].

Codification, quality assurance and the demands of accountability

In Chapter 7, I explore the tensions between cultures of creativity and cultures of audit and accountability, in the context of leadership. This is also a lived tension in the professional identity of the teacher-artist, clear from Jo Parkes' account in Chapter 4 of the struggles over autonomy, purpose and the place in the organisation's mission of the *Home* project. To understand how innovative projects such as *Home* challenge accepted institutional and organisational frames of mind, Peter Renshaw's distinction between 'tacit' and 'explicit' knowledge is helpful:

> In any arts institution there is an inevitable tension between tacit and explicit knowledge. For instance, the demands of Quality Assurance necessitate that knowledge and procedures are formulated and conveyed explicitly in the public domain. Yet much of the energy, immediacy, spontaneity and creativity central to artistic processes are rooted in a form of life in which knowledge and awareness are more implicit than explicit. Finding ways of managing the apparent paradox between [measured] Quality and quality, and between explicit and tacit knowledge, is critical to the future work of higher arts education institutions. Conversations involving artists and teachers are absolutely essential if the integrity of artistic engagement is not to be destroyed. (Renshaw, 2003, p13)

As the management structure of the college changed between 1996 and 2004, longer-standing members of the team became acutely aware of how many of the key practices which underpinned our ways of working were not embedded in the explicit, written organisational systems of the institution. This created a tension between the actual working practices of the team, transmitted through an oral and relatively informal culture of collaboration and partnership, and the formal written procedures and systems of the college which barely recognised the existing innovations. Tensions grew between the unwritten knowledge and expertise of the teaching team and the legislative knowledge and procedures required by the institution and its broader context of funding and accountability requirements.

The team struggled to establish the acceptability of their ways of working within the broader context of college systems and procedures, especially after keen advocates in the senior management team left the college. The question remained: were the creativity, flexibility and the creative teaching and learning mechanisms described in these pages only the icing on a corporate cake? Or could they be embedded and made core to the operational systems and ways of thinking of the college as a whole and be supported as a core activity and not merely something it was nice to have.[5] Without wholehearted commitment to the work by the institution's senior leadership and a commitment to organisational adaptation and learning from the work, the staff were always going to feel that their work was marginal and risky. And yet the benefits for students in terms of achievement, progression and personal development were perfectly obvious.

Renshaw also points out that the communicative power of the arts to shock, move or change public perceptions depends on the nurturing of energy, immersiveness, immediacy and spontaneity. These values and attributes feel alien to some of the bureaucratic and prescriptive models of regulation and accountability in education. Conflict and difficulty may provoke creativity; the effort to problem-solve and find new solutions is creative. But it is important to work in an organisational climate which allows enough autonomy to develop creative solutions. All our case studies tell of teachers' difficulties and struggles to reconcile complex and frequently contradictory demands. Heavy-handed and insensitive approaches to management, accountability and leadership – what Charles Landry (2000, p54) calls 'box-like, bi-polar, or compartmentalised thinking' – can stifle creativity before it has a chance to take root. This applies as much to the leadership of teams of teachers as it does to teachers' roles as leaders of their students' learning.

I am not arguing that skills acquisition in arts processes should be abandoned in favour of a generalised creativity. In this book we explore models of arts education that move beyond the binary divide that has separated traditionalists, who place more emphasis on developing skills training within established repertoires, and progressives, who tend to be concerned more with investigation, social interaction and the value of the transferable skills engendered in arts practices. A critical and questioning orientation to the development of skills, knowledge and inventiveness is needed, that allows time and space for learners to research, investigate and present their work. Margaret Boden (in Craft *et al*, 2001, p102) puts it like this:

> Creativity and knowledge are two sides of the same psychological coin, not opposing forces... Creativity is not the same thing as knowledge, but is firmly grounded in it. What educators must try to do is to nurture the knowledge without killing the creativity.

Reclaiming – and reconstructing – professionalism

For models of teacher identity like those described here are to gain ground, a 'transformative professionalism' may be required. Judyth Sachs believes this depends upon

> ...a collective strategy on the part of those engaged in any educational enterprise. It means that new forms of work organisation are established between teachers, in particular that the hoary chestnut of teacher privatism, isolation and individualism is dispensed with... Identifying with transformative professionalism means that teachers will have to work collaboratively, not only with other teachers but also with others interested in education and improving student learning... (Sachs, 2003a, p15)

One key location[6] where this new type of professionalism might be developed is at the arts and education interface. Creative partnership opens up opportunities to work collaboratively and may challenge established notions of where and how teaching and learning takes place. There need to be clear values and priorities that govern choices about partnership development. Dialogue is required not only between individual members of staff but also between wider college systems and corporate strategies, and the ways of working adopted by its partners.

Teacher as activist or social entrepreneur

Sachs argues that accountability and autonomy should not be regarded as utterly incompatible, unless the notion of teaching as a 'profession' is to be completely discarded. She argues that transformative professionalism includes the following features:

- Inclusive membership
- A public ethical code of practice
- Collaborative and collegial

- Activist orientation
- Flexible and progressive
- Responsive to change
- Self regulating
- Policy-active
- Enquiry orientated
- Knowledge building (Sachs, 2003, p16)

Sachs maintains that an activist frame of mind allows teachers to construct professional identities that are 'based on democratic principles, negotiated, collaborative, socially critical, future-oriented, strategic and tactical (2003a, p134). She identifies a managerialist discourse of educational reform as fostering 'an entrepreneurial identity in which the market and issues of accountability, economy, efficiency and effectiveness shape how teachers individually and collectively construct their professional identities.' She argues instead for democratic discourses of reform which would 'support an activist professional identity in which collaborative cultures are an intrinsic part of teachers' work practices' (Sachs, 2003a, p134).

The notion of the 'social entrepreneur' (Leadbeater, 1997) or 'learning broker' (LSDA, 2004) suggest possible ways of understanding how an activist teacher might make use of collaborative working to construct new pathways and opportunities for learning, but Sachs regards entrepreneurialism as too heavily tainted by market ideologies to be useful. Quoting Casey (1995), she criticises ' 'designer employees' who consistently demonstrate compliance to policy imperatives and perform at high levels of efficiency and effectiveness' (2003a, p128). If entrepreneurship is mainly about gaining competitive advantage, then within managerialist educational discourse 'competition between schools for scarce resources gives rise to a competitive ethos rather than a collaborative one', set within a Standards regime 'which professes to drive up standards – but is really about the 'standardisation' of practice' (p 128-129). And standardisation of practice, she suggests, leads to standardisation of teaching styles and a sense of disempowerment and loss of autonomy within the profession.

> In order to 'meet the Standards' you have to be the kind of person that the standards have in mind, capable of accomplishing the activities that the Standards entail, living with and constructing the relationships presumed at different levels, and of working within the assumptions which form the Standards boundaries. (Mahony and Hextall, 2000, p79)

According to Sachs, entrepreneurial identity is 'individualistic, competitive, controlling and regulative, externally defined, and standards led' (2003a, p130).

Using the term entrepreneur does have risky connotations for a profession which has at its heart the idea of public service and welfare, but I would strongly contest the idea that developing forms of entrepreneurship within the profession is entirely negative. The word enterprise has a number of derivations – from *entre-prise*, to prise apart or break open; and from *entre-prendere* or *emprendre*, to take – which implies a notion of reclamation and innovation, embarking on an undertaking that requires initiative and risk-taking. The notion of 'breaking up' or 'splitting apart' is also not far from the surface of enterprise culture[7], and this understandably causes anxiety in a profession which, historically, carries important traditions of social solidarity, social justice and the 'common good' (see Carr and Hartnett, 1996). Entrepreneurship involves exploiting existing resources, spotting opportunities and creating new products and services out of what exists. Developing new teaching practices and new forms of teachers' work appropriate to teaching and learning in the 21st Century will require innovation. And if this is not to be entirely centrally driven, the profession needs to find ways of making it happen.

> Social entrepreneurs mobilise under-utilised resources, people and buildings written off by business or the formal education system to meet unmet social needs. Social entrepreneurs' assets are mainly the relationships they build with their clients, staff, partners and funders. Their output is entirely intangible: goodwill, trust, confidence and security. Yet these are not do-gooders. They are entrepreneurs: driven, determined, ambitious and creative. Successful social entrepreneurs are good leaders. They are very good at setting a mission for an organisation and mobilising people around it... That is why they are good storytellers... The best entrepreneurial social organisations are porous at the edges. (Leadbeater, 2000, p213)

The heroic status of the entrepreneur in New Labour politics may still be open to question, especially when, in a business context, that entrepreneur is permitted to disregard established social entitlements and environmental safeguards in the name of 'innovation.' But there is no doubt that the entrepreneur – rather like the artist as described by Carol Becker, and increasingly celebrated in the 'new economy' as the 'creative' entrepreneur – looms large in public consciousness as the innovative outsider, the risk-taker or the alchemist (Handy, 1999). The social entrepreneur is regarded as someone who acts in the public or community interest rather than primarily for private profit – even though they undoubtedly reap personal rewards and satisfaction from their ways of working[8]. Their work is seen as creating social inventions which build value, providing services to communities in engaging and involving ways. People who find the notion of the social market appealing as a 'third way' see the social entrepreneur as creating 'social capital' which, according to Putnam (2001), provides the social glue to help revitalise fragmented communities. The validity of the notion of social capital (see Fine, 2000; Baron *et al*, 2001) is not the issue here. I use the term social entrepreneur in relation to teachers' work for pragmatic and rhetorical purposes, to reclaim the territory of entrepreneurship for the public good.

As Leadbeater points out, the governance of large public sector institutions differs from that of small voluntary sector organisations. It takes considerable political skill and organisational will to achieve the flexibility and devolved control necessary to sustain innovation. The education service has an ambivalent relationship with enterprise culture, not least because of resistance to market values and the proposition that educational values should be driven by the perceived needs of the economy (Ecclestone, 2002; Apple and Beane, 1999). But the notion of social entrepreneurship as a form of recuperation and reclamation may be a legitimate tactic for activist teachers to take control over their work. Our case studies strongly indicate that such forms of work can be experienced as empowering, exciting, rewarding and progressive[9].

Teaching, leadership, citizenship

According to Andy Hargreaves (2003, p2-3), teachers are caught in a triple bind:

- ■ To be the catalysts of the knowledge society and all the opportunity and prosperity it promises to bring

- ■ To be the counterpoints to the knowledge society and its threats to inclusiveness, security and public life

- ■ To be the casualties of the knowledge society in a world where escalating expectations for education are being met with standardised solutions, provided at minimum cost

On one hand, teachers have to deal with the rhetoric and realities of a fast-moving, network-y knowledge society, and on the other, they operate within learning institutions, governmental funding and accountability frameworks that work quite differently. They are subject to strong centralised control and to intense inspection and criticism of their work. 'Quality systems' provide the means to validate claims to competence and value, but they also provide technologies of intervention, surveillance and control, arguably threatening civil society's frameworks of trust and self-regulation within the professional sphere (Strathern, 2000; O'Neill, 2002). The value systems, assumptions and even the communicative style through which such cultures of quality control operate – at the level of the team, the institution, and the wider regulatory system – determine whether the teacher feels empowered or undermined.

To use Raymond Williams' phrase, there is a sense in which the institutional frameworks of audit and accountability within which teachers operate translate into 'structures of feeling'. All too often mechanisms of 'accountability' precipitate stress, anxiety, fragmentation and competition between staff. Emphasising collaboration and mutuality and speaking in terms of team working and collegiality shifts accountability and management into the appropriate preserve of the professional community.

The ideology of teamwork

The notion of teamwork and collaboration as underpinning the ability of teachers to develop, respect and respond to the autonomy of learners, building communities based on shared values of social justice[9] is not new. It is forcefully articulated in the literature surrounding the development of more radical, democratic models of comprehensive education[10] during the 1970s and 1980s in institutions such as the Leicestershire community colleges and Stantonbury Campus (see for example Moon, 1983; Glatter, 1989; Jensen and Walker, 1989) and in the US (Apple and Beane, 1999).

In this model, expanded team structures of teachers who bring together different areas of learning in broader groupings, replace the traditional hierarchies of departments divided by subjects with strict ladders of management responsibility. The notion of team working is a powerful device in contemporary management theory[11] to encourage the sharing of responsibility for knowledge generation and management; the rhetoric of 'collaboration' replaces 'competition' as the stated core dynamic.

Richard Sennett is critical of the ideology of teamwork. He suggests that these rhetorics lead to the exercise by managers of 'power without responsibility' – 'teamwork' becomes a euphemism for exerting power over groups of workers, bouncing back accountability and responsibility into 'teams'. These teams usually are paid less than their managers, who can indulge in buck-passing, abdication of responsibility, blame and manipulation.[12] A member of the arts and media team memorably described NewVIc as 'the

IKEA of the FE world'. At NewVIc the rhetoric of teamwork and collaboration sits alongside a demanding and target-driven senior management style in which decision-making, whilst shared to an extent, relies heavily on a professed 'informality'. This can result in a lack of transparency, clarity, and managers' accountability *to* their teams. The sense of where the actual decision-making power in the organisation rests can be elusive. As in many similar institutions, there are tensions between what Sachs (2003b) might define as managerialist and democratic/collaborative discourses.

Teamwork needs to be underpinned by a framework of shared values which allow staff to collaborate in a spirit of mutual support and trust (see Fielding, 1999; Sachs, 2003b). If there is a commitment to social justice, to equality and reciprocity with learners and staff, there has to be openness and honesty about the different power relationships at work. Moving relationships with outside agencies beyond one-off encounters and short-term projects required strategic thinking about the changes needed to curriculum, timetable and use of spaces. These new ways of working were rarely mirrored elsewhere in the college.

Just who was doing the most strategic thinking – junior members of staff or senior management – caused some tension. In traditional hierarchical institutions, there is a clear distinction made between strategy – the preserve of the senior management – and operations, the preserve of the frontline staff. In the work of the arts and media team these boundaries were blurred. The partnership-led nature of the work demanded that strategic thinking become a joint activity between managers and staff, not a top-down imposition. The capacity of the college to support new initiatives and the strong encouragement from senior managers in the early years of the work helped to build the foundations for the current web of relationships.

A team can claim to have made a relationship when more than one of its members is involved in it; it can claim to have sustained a relationship when the work with another organisation moves beyond a single collaboration into something longer-term. Once staff from the arts and media team began to be seconded to other organisations or satellite projects – first Stratford Circus, then the Circus Media creative business support project, and lastly the University of East London – the question arose of who should manage staff who were working across organisational boundaries and had multiple accountabilities.

Because organisational autonomy and control are lost when taking on a partner to deliver a service, partnership working can be a high risk strategy for a well-resourced institution. The people who work across the boundaries of institutions and organisations are important as intermediaries who interpret and translate between different institutional cultures. And they can also act as gatekeepers, making decisions about who can gain access to the resources of each organisation.

Intermediaries and gatekeepers are valuable, but only if they are acting in accordance with shared values of the team and the broader organisational context. Who defines what these values are and how are gatekeepers and intermediaries held accountable?

An ethics of accountability

Within our expanded learning and teaching landscape, the foundations of professional accountability need to remain in place, so that activities undertaken in the frame of creative partnership retain currency and legitimacy as valid educational experiences. The teacher as artist, activist or social entrepreneur must never abdicate the fundamental principle of altruism in the focus on learning, progression and empowerment. How is this work going to benefit learners and assist them to achieve their potential?

Bottery (1996) suggests five ethical principles for teachers working in the context of the 'new public management':

- ■ An ethic of truth disclosure which must override personal advantage

- ■ An ethic of subjectivity, for each individual must recognise the limits of his or her perceptions, the individuality of his or her values

- ■ An ethic of reflective integrity as each professional recognises the limits of personal perception, of the need to incorporate many understandings of a situation

- ■ An ethic of humility as each professional recognises that such subjectivity means that personal fallibility is not a failing but a condition of being human

- ■ An ethic of humanistic education: of the duty to help the client help themselves (Bottery, 1996, p193)

Creative partnership based upon clear ethical principles has proved to unlock considerable potential. We may not need a quasi-legislative approach to partnership like the Urban Missions community arts partnership programme at Columbia College in Chicago, which has adopted a system of 'bye-laws' to govern its operation. However, emergent value-frameworks need to be openly discussed and shared between the chief actors in partnership management and also right across organisations. Only within a strong ethical framework in which the partners trust one another – whether trust is implicit, embedded in practice or written and codified – can collaboration and partnership operate effectively.

Personal consequences and effects

The blurring of boundaries has personal as well as professional effects. Staff found that the balance between their professional work and their personal lives was severely challenged at times. The demands of organisational working that required explanation, dialogue and constantly refining aims were draining. The bleeding of the work into weekends and evenings became increasingly hard to sustain.

Sid Hughes described his view of staff development and why he saw it as important to support the team in developing this way of working:

> I always felt that teachers ought to be able to differentiate their portfolio of experience, interests and skills, just as a student should be encouraged to do... Teachers as learners should be encouraged to widen their portfolio so that their point of entry into the college might not be the point that they find themselves at three years down the line... When they're leaving they should go out with far more than they come in with. And I always felt it would be a good idea that people could have some teaching of 16-19, some teaching with adults, involvement in some project development work... a variety of different things that they could do, would be interested in doing, or would be very good at doing... But it's not always easy to really either explain the value of that in the longer term, or to encourage people to do it... I always [thought], from a teacher's point of view, that was something that would safeguard their job in a college when jobs were at risk. If you were teaching just one thing and put all your eggs in that particular basket, and that particular basket split, you've had it. Whereas if you are teaching across a variety of different things you become quite indispensable. And you also become a very strong candidate for another post elsewhere because your level of expertise has been developed. (interview transcript, 2002)

This management philosophy is very person-centred, as it understands that people have to be persuaded of the value of these approaches, and that psychological investment must be made in them for them to succeed. Such a philosophy has considerable strengths because it allows individuals to pursue their own learning journeys within the framework of the college. And it recognises that the organisation is only as effective as the individuals who make it work, and that developing teachers as learners is one of the foundations for success. But it also pushes much of the responsibility for these learning journeys onto individuals and teams, and as Sennett (1998) warns, may lead to an abdication of responsibility or accountability for the management of new initiatives by people not wholly invested in the innovative models of working.

Towards an empowering culture

This chapter has argued that a reconstructed notion of teacher professional identity to support a networked curriculum for arts learning requires the re-examination of

- the roles and relationships between teachers and artists in creative partnership

- the cultures, styles and characteristics of leadership and accountability operating at all levels in the education system, and how they might inhibit creative approaches

- whether the teacher could usefully be conceptualised as artist-activist or social entrepreneur, and which models of learning organisations could support teachers of this kind

All these principles need further research, refinement and testing in different educational contexts. This book does not explore the potential applicability of these models of partnership in curriculum areas such as the humanities, or business, technology and science education, but there may be grounds for dialogue. The UK's Creative Partnerships initiative has not restricted its approaches to arts education. Rather, like the NACCCE report (1999) from which it came, it seeks to address the issue of creativity across the whole school curriculum.

Traditions of comprehensive education and certain established practices in further and higher education have always placed an emphasis on the importance of teacher as researcher, as practitioner, or even as community activist, extending their direct vocational experience and enhancing their curriculum expertise. The rhetoric of lifelong learning also increasingly requires educational institutions to extend their activities into community engagement, regeneration, business support and cross-sector partnership.

In these expanded contexts for arts educators, successful learning in and through the arts requires:

- the notion of reflective practice, and *making time* for it

- collaborative cultures and supportive leadership and management

- that artistic skills are modelled within a wider, inclusive network of collaborative relationships, based on shared values, among a broad pool of expertise – professional artists, mentors, arts and cultural organisations

Tension and conflict between not just individuals and organisational systems but also centrally determined policy frameworks and the organisation of learning, are a virtually inevitable consequence of commitment to creativity. Finding ways to live with contradictions (see MacBeath, 2003) and managing complexity, may mean that living 'on the edge of chaos' becomes the only constant among the skills required of creative professionals. The tensions are necessary. They can bring about individual and organisational change:

> When a member of a bureaucracy embarks on a course of reflective practice, allowing himself to experience confusion and uncertainty, subjecting his frames and theories to conscious criticism and change, he may increase his capacity to contribute to significant organisational learning, but he also becomes, by the same token, a danger to the stable system of rules and procedures within which he is expected to deliver his technical expertise. (Schön, 1983, p328)

Lawrence Stenhouse suggests even more radical consequences may confront institutions of learning if the notion of teacher as artist/researcher takes hold:

> What are the consequences of such a movement if it gains momentum and power? May we expect teachers to demand schools fit for educational artist-researchers to live in? And what would these look like?

> We can only guess. But I am suggesting that forms of schooling can best be seen as obsolescent when they constrict developments in teaching. I believe that the development of teacher as artist means that some time in the future we are going to have to get rid of school principals. My own guess is that we will need delegatory rather than legislative democracy. (1986, p109)

Notes

1 See Schön, 1983; Craft, 1997; Gale and Densmore, 2000.

2 Animarts (2003, p43-44) provides a lexicon of attributes needed for skilled facilitation. These could apply equally to a teacher or artist's facilitation of creative process, but Animarts uses them to describe some of the 'professional characteristics' of the animateur.

Animarts tends to fall back on a 'separate but equal' status for teacher and artist. I argue for a more subtle definition which involves a *design* perspective, on the collaborative design of learning experiences between teachers and artists.

3   We observed this process at first hand in the ways in which Mark Murphy, Chris Devaney, Dominic Murcott and their skilled team in Vtol Dance Company took our BTEC students through an entire devising and performance-making process in the month-long *Running Scared* project at Trinity Buoy Wharf in 1998 (see www.vtol.co.uk). At the time, Mark Murphy observed that: 'It would be an easier route to arrive at such a project with a fixed approach and the assured knowledge of a safe outcome. The much harder, and ultimately more satisfying choice, is to risk all by making a collaborative pieces which evolves from the students' own life experiences, and views the process as importantly as the finished work' (from programme note for *Running Scared,* 1998).

4   The work undertaken by London International Festival of Theatre (www.liftfest.org) has offered catalytic opportunities to educators across the city for 23 years. LIFT operates a kind of organisational thinking, commissioning and developing new artistic work in which the notion of theatre and festival is explored and exploded in an interventionist and un-settling way.

5   Interestingly this mirrors some research into policymakers, funders and awardees' perceptions of barriers to realising creative ideas in the UK, undertaken by NESTA (see ICM, 2002).

6   Other key loci of collaboration currently affecting teacher professional identities in the UK include education-business partnerships, the 14-19 agenda, Extended Schools and health and citizenship education, crime diversion crime prevention, and proposals contained in the 2003 Children's Act for more collaborative working between agencies charged with child protection. The impact of education policies which require partnership are explored further in Chapter 7 and in Powell, Glendinning and Rummery (2002).

7   See Strathern (2000, p288): 'New forms of managerial government... are the outcome of policy measures on the part of specific governments, reinforced by a corporate community which gives them international credibility. For these outcomes have involved the deliberate promotion of key concepts and this, as a matter of policy, deliberate attempts to modify people's cultural outlooks. [See] ...Shore and Wright (1997), which argues that 'policy' should be of great interest to anthropological enquiry as an arena where governments re-invent society and promote cultural change. This they point to a cluster of 'keywords' developed in the UK – but not restricted to it – during the New Right discourse of the 1980s. It embedded certain conceptualisations of the individual (person) in a nexus including 'freedom', 'market', 'enterprise' and 'family' (1997, p19-29). The constellation was quite deliberately put together, in Marquand's (1992, p69) words, as part of the Thatcherite project to limit the role of the state: 'Neo-liberals hold that the market is the realm of freedom, and the state the realm of coercion.' 'Enterprise culture' summed it up at the time.'

8   See also Csikszentmihalyi, 2003, and Gardner, Csikszentmihalyi and Damon, 2001 on 'Good Work'.

9   Lingard *et al*: social justice as 'a politics which positively engages with difference and for one that is concerned with matters of (re)distribution' (2002, p29). See also Young, 1990, 1997; Gale and Densmore, 2000; and Harvey, 1988.

10   see Harber, 1992; O'Hagan, 1991 and Meighan and Toogood, 1992.

11   see for example, Senge, 1990; Wenger, 1999; Fisher and Fisher, 1998; Deprez and Tissen, 2002.

12   Sennett, 1998 pp114-116: 'the fiction that workers and management are on the same team... [Such] fictions of teamwork, because of their very superficiality of content and

focus on the immediate moment, their avoidance of resistance and deflection of con-frontation, are thus useful in the exercise of domination...The manager who declares that we are all victims of time and place is perhaps the most cunning figure to appear in the pages of this book. He has mastered the art of wielding power without being held accountable; he has transcended that responsibility for himself, putting the ills of work back on the shoulders of those fellow 'victims' who happen to work for him.'

6

Collaboration or collapse?
NewVIc and the Stratford
Cultural Quarter

Andrew Blake

A collaborative project

This chapter explores the ways in which higher education and business support the performing arts at NewVIc. Because of how this provision was delivered, it also discusses the developing – and at the time of the assessment challenging – relationship with the Stratford Circus arts centre.[1]

Arts in the community: the political and economic context

The New Labour government was quick to rename the Department for National Heritage the Department for Culture, Media and Sport (DCMS). As the title implies the new ministry had a wide brief, but the overall objective was to strengthen the contribution of these areas of life to the national economy. The post-World War Two settlement had funded a high-culture sector which claimed to be above commerce: the arts were intrinsically good, produced by well-trained and gifted people for the rest of us to enjoy, and should be paid for accordingly. But the new Government saw things rather differently. In their 1997 manifesto they declared that:

> Art, sport and leisure industries are vital to our quality of life and the renewal of our economy. They are significant earners for Britain. They employ hundreds of thousands of people (www.labour.org.uk, accessed 5.5.97).

Thus the new government called 'the creative industries' into existence, seeing them as simultaneously a sign of modernity, an export earner, and a provider of work which might even interest people from disadvantaged areas. In 1998 the DCMS produced a creative industries mapping document auditing these activities, and updated it in 2001. Through a raft of policies such as the 'new deal' for musicians, and the requirement for all local authorities to produce culture-for-inclusion policies of their own in the form of Local Cultural Strategies, the government sought to reinforce the message that culture-as-industry was a viable way of modernising both society and the economy alike.

Even the principal distributor of high-culture subsidy, Arts Council England, reinvented itself as an agency which had social inclusion and the celebration of diversity among its aims, and was rewarded with far more funds.[2] Subsequent debates within government and its think-tank hinterland, however, have indicated that even as the arts try to represent themselves as vehicles for social inclusion, celebration of multicultural and diverse Britain, and economic prosperity[3], there is still room for an old-fashioned view of 'culture' as the best that has been thought and said, provided for most people by the extravagantly gifted.[4]

The Mayor of London responded to this wide-ranging agenda with a draft policy document mapping out the capital's cultural goals. These were firmed up in *London – Cultural Capital*, published in April 2004. Four aspects of the emergent policy are worth noting:

■ 'The creative and cultural industries need to be recognised as a significant contributor to London's economy and success'[5]... In an area dominated by self-employment and small companies, support structures need to be established for small businesses and to nurture new talent .

■ 'Education and lifelong learning must play a central role in nurturing creativity and providing routes to employment'[6]... Black and minority ethnic groups, and people with disabilities, may need more support to gain the education, training or experience to fill the many jobs in the cultural sector... [we will] explore ways of using major new cultural developments to maximise opportunities for Black, Asian and minority ethnic groups.[7]

■ 'There should be a spread of high-quality cultural provision across London and at all levels – local, sub-regional and regional'... [The Mayor should] facilitate strategic partnerships to maximise growth of cultural provision – co-ordinating development to the east as a new area of growth.[8]

- ■ 'Cultural quarters must be developed as key contributors to London's creative capital and the development of the broader economy... [as] achieving a better balance between the cultural facilities of inner and outer London can go some way towards reducing the social and economic inequalities between different parts of the city. [The Mayor should] support the development of cultural quarters and promote their role in regeneration, encouraging creative industry developments in the Thames Gateway region.'[9]

To achieve these economic and social goals education was part of the DCMS brief. In September 2002, for example, the Secretary of State for Education launched Creative Partnerships, jointly sponsored by DCMS and the Department for Education and Skills (DfES), to involve professional arts practitioners working with schoolchildren from 'deprived coastal, rural and urban areas in England'.[10] The government's key 1997 election pledge had been to improve education provision and to widen participation. The two concerns were brought together in the creation of the National Endowment for Science, Technology and the Arts (NESTA), which is overseen by DCMS. Using an endowment from the National Lottery (also overseen by DCMS), NESTA has supported projects in education and invested in individual innovators, as well as other kinds of applied research, in order 'to provide a real boost to the UK's economic, cultural and creative capital'.[11]

Lottery funds transformed the work of the Arts Council. It is perhaps too easy to fund capital projects for new or restored buildings far but harder to fund the running of them, despite changes to the Lottery's rules in 1998 which made better allocation for revenue funding, salaries etc, rather than just capital projects. A number of Lottery-funded projects have failed, such as the flagship National Centre for Popular Music which opened in Sheffield in March 1999 and was closed in June 2000, because of poor attendance. The building was sold in 2002 to Sheffield Hallam University for its Student Union. The Arts Council had allocated £11 million of Lottery capital funding for the project but it had no charge over the building and recouped only about £40,000 from the sale. A 2003 National Audit Office report into capital projects funded by Arts Council England recommended that 'the Arts Council should apply without exception its policy of securing a legal charge on any asset funded with lottery money so that public money is protected in the event of projects failing'.[12]

Arts centres, cultural industry and education

Given the politically driven roles of education and culture in the regeneration of local economies and communities, it is unsurprising that arts centres which have survived and prospered or look likely to do so have embarked on ambitious but synergistic relationships. Models are emerging of Arts Council and local council collaboration in using the arts centre as a nexus of provision for education, small business and artist support, as well as professional performance. These include[13]:

■ *Dovecot Arts Centre, Stockton-on-Tees*, which received £7.5 million of Arts Council/Lottery support. It opened in 2000, failed to meet projected revenue targets, and closed in November 2001. The venue was rescued, its mission was reinvented, and it was renamed and reopened in 2003 as The Arc. It has since been given wholehearted local council support and funding alongside continuing Arts Council support.[14] The Arc is home to professional theatre, music, comedy, dance and films; amateur and community events such as the annual three day local music industry convention for all aspirants; regular showcase nights for unsigned bands; creative writing classes; and links with local SMEs.[15] Education collaborations with Stockton Riverside College – one of two centres of vocational excellence in performing arts in the UK – and the University of Teesside make it an active location for those learning the trade as well as professionals. Its Café Scientifique, set up in collaboration with a University of Durham outpost, gives audiences a point of contact with the wider intellectual and commercial world.[16]

■ *The Sage Gateshead*, opened in 2004, is housed in a purpose-built building on the south bank of the River Tyne designed by Norman Foster. Owned by Gateshead Council and supported by the largest ever Arts Lottery grant given outside London, the Sage plans to present leading British and international artists in classical, popular and vernacular musics, and to develop an equal partnership between performance, education and community programmes. The two resident ensembles, Northern Sinfonia and Folkworks, will deliver performance and education projects through a mix of tours, concerts, festivals, workshops, Summer Schools, weekly, weekend and one-day courses and work in schools and colleges. Folkworks has recently collaborated with Newcastle University on a pioneering degree course in Traditional Musics.

■ *The Folkestone cultural quarter*, funded in part by Saga Holidays boss Roger de Haan, plans to include higher education provision via Kent Institute of Art and Design and Canterbury Christ Church University College, and under-18 education from a City Academy in the Arts being built to open in 2006. The town's Creative Foundation, which is overseeing the development of the creative quarter, has been given £620K by Arts Council England, South East for the renovation of town centre property which will be let to artists and creative businesses at below-market rents.[17]

■ The redevelopment of the *Broadway Theatre, Barking*, is a partnership between London Borough of Barking and Dagenham and Barking College School of Performing Arts, with funding from the Council and the College, the Learning and Skills Council, Barking Town Centre Partnership and the London Development Agency. The Theatre, reopened in late 2004, boasts a flexible auditorium suitable for music, dance or drama. The basement houses an education suite of dance, music, stage craft, recording, drama and technology rooms, for the use of Barking College School of Performing Arts. The Theatre is in Barking Town Centre, a site identified for cultural and social regeneration as part of the Thames Gateway Development. It forms part of the borough's ambitions for a cultural hub mixing artists' studios, a lifelong learning centre, and library and exhibition facilities. To this end, the nearby Malthouse building has been refurbished to provide workspaces for cultural industries and arts groups, and the adjoining site has been bought by the London Development Agency.

■ The London Development Agency has also acquired *Three Mills Studios*, a busy film and television studio complex in Newham. The studios will be managed by the LDA with the advice of industry body Film London. Tony Winterbottom, director of regeneration and development at the LDA, said: 'The LDA has acquired Three Mills studios as part of its ongoing commitment to develop the capital's creative strengths through its Creative London project. We announced in April [2004] at the launch of Creative London that we were going to set up ten creative hubs providing flexible workspace and support facilities. Three Mills will form a key part of east London's creative hub.'[18]

As the latter two examples indicate, there is fierce competition for the cultural-regeneration pound, and there may already be too many arts centres in east London fighting both for the same slices of public funding and for similar markets in potential resident artists, students and audiences. Nonetheless any working model which manages to combine education, community provision, local business support and professional performance is probably more likely to succeed in the current climate. The collaborative relationship between the resident organisations at Stratford Circus and NewVIc is one such model.

NewVIc and higher education in East London

NewVIc has historic strategic aims to:

- be an inclusive, stimulating and highly successful learning environment

- achieve maximum levels of progression to college and from college to continuing education and careers

- support local businesses and contribute to the economic regeneration of the community

To which was added in 2001 that regeneration of the locality was increasingly important, and that the college's 'business unit has made a major contribution to local regeneration bids.'[19]

Performing arts provision, although slow to grow in the first few years, has become a significant part of NewVIc's success; the arts and media team won three Beacon awards in 1998-2002. Work in dance, drama and music has been developed by skilled and dedicated practitioners who have tried to think innovatively about their work as teacher-practitioners, and also to think beyond the College, curriculum and classroom to develop their work within the wider community. The arts team has made itself part of the local hub of thinking about culture, creativity and regeneration and was therefore consonant with local and central governmental thinking on these issues.

In November 1998, for example, NewVIc organised a conference entitled 'Arts Partnerships in Newham – a way forward'. It invited all the organisations in the Borough working in the arts, as well as all drama and dance teachers and several local artists. Fifty delegates wanted the Council to adopt a strategic and dynamic creative and cultural policy. They felt that such a policy should be congruent with the existing policies of all Council departments, particularly education and regeneration. The policy should, delegates argued, have three mutually supporting elements:

- A set of goals adopted by the Council to promote arts and creative development in Newham for cultural and commercial reasons, consistent with leisure, education, economic development and regeneration policy.

- An open, cross-sectoral, fully representative Creative Forum embracing a broad range of people, from arts practitioners to educators and workers in creative industries and including the Council as a key partner.

- Projects developed through this partnership to develop artistic practice and participation, commercial exploitation of creative and cultural resources, and education in support of both.

NewVIc and Urban Development have since sought to formulate a Newham music development partnership through which some of these goals might be addressed. There is an aspiration to 'join up' arts provision in the borough for people at all life stages and levels of achievement through the central provision of information and development of networks of organisations, individual artists and creative professionals.[20]

Supra-institutional strategic thinking of this kind led to NewVIc's development of higher education provision in partnership with UEL. This provision, set within the Circus, has been able to effect precisely the innovative mixture of education, regeneration and entertainment which is implied in the aims of both local and central government policy.

Collaboration – and collapse

From the mid-1990s, Newham Council and Stratford Development Partnership brought together a consortium of organisations to develop a new cultural quarter in Stratford. The centrepiece was to be a new performing arts centre and a refurbished and extended Theatre Royal, Stratford East. Building on a distinguished history of developing participation in arts activity in terms of both audience and performers from working class and Black and Asian communities – work pioneered by Joan Littlewood and Theatre Workshop from the 1940s onwards (Coren, 1984) – the vision for the cultural quarter was one in which popular entertainment and a revitalised night-time economy for Stratford would sit alongside education, training and employment opportunities for local people.

Stratford Circus, the centre point of the proposed cultural quarter, was built using £14 million of National Lottery funding delivered by Arts Council England, alongside £1.4 million from English Partnerships and City Challenge. This was a serious investment and statement of confidence in the development potential of arts organisations in what was then the second most deprived borough in Britain. From 1998 the staff for Salway Arts Ltd, the company which would run the new venue, began to be appointed. Each of the core partners had a seat on the board of the new company, along with representatives from the local authority, Stratford Development Partnership and the wider community of stakeholders. A pre-opening programme was developed, the core partners collaborating to create a number of successful events designed to attract audiences and participants ahead of the opening. Clare Connor of NewVIc and Tony Coleman of NEWCEYS were seconded to the new organisation to form its Education department. Working with Kiki Gale of East London Dance and the staff of Theatre Venture, they began developing models of collaborative project design. Pre-programming included internationally acclaimed work such as the *Flower Eyes* project with Suburo Teshigawara and Karas, locally driven pilot arts in health initiatives, *Bedtime Stories*, an opera involving around 40 older Newham residents, and *Mixed Doubles Match Point*, a project exploring the duet in dance with artists and young people from east London colleges.

Because of budget over-runs the specification of the building was downgraded several times, the most significant loss being a rehearsal space which would have physically connected the Circus building with the adjacent Theatre Royal. Alongside the Theatre Royal, in which the original auditorium was left intact but all technical, administrative and front of house facilities were extensively remodelled, Stratford Circus opened in the autumn of 2001, nine months behind schedule. Within its glass and steel frame are two main performance spaces: a courtyard theatre with flytower and full-scale proscenium stage for dance, theatre and music of all kinds, and a spacious studio theatre. It has a large dance rehearsal studio, bars, meeting rooms and multi media facilities. Sprung floors, flexible staging and audience spaces, state-of-the-art sound and lighting made the building an attractive venue for performance, teaching and conferences.

The principle of interchange and flexibility between spaces was built in from the beginning, but unfortunately the organisational, financial and administrative systems needed to make this model of multiple and overlapping usage work were not. The first two years of the Circus's existence as a commercial venue were financially disastrous. Programming was mixed and unfocused. It included much fringe drama, right next door to an established theatre, so houses were small and revenue negligible. Partners were involved in constant tussles with the venue managers over the vision, purpose and direction of the building. The original business plan had assumed that the venue would run on a one-third subsidy, two-thirds earned income model – which the Arts Council did not expect of even arts centres in affluent parts of London.

Individual programming successes included work presented by Shobana Jeyasingh, Robert Hylton, Akram Khan, CandoCo Dance Company, Union Dance, Soul II Soul, Terri Walker and Shaun Escoffery. But they were eclipsed by disputes between the partners and the building's management over operational systems and about who was responsible for snagging the building's faults. There was little clarity about systems for decision-making, accountability, space booking, or marketing and development.

The day-to-day operation of the building was funded by a consortium led by Newham Council, which had released funds on the expectation that NewVIc and the other core partners[21] were not only involved in the programming of the projects within the building, but also had defined contractual relationships with those administering the Circus itself. In fact, no contracts were ever signed. Perhaps because of the lack of contracts or any substitute such as service level agreements or documented relations of right and responsibility, early relationships between Circus management and core partners were unsatisfactory. Despite the bankrolling of the new centre by funds from NewVIc and the core partners, through the design of collaborative projects which provided revenue funding to underpin the building's running costs as well as funding for project delivery, the management of the Circus seemed to see the core partners – and many of the other users of the building – as a necessary inconvenience. Certainly it did not see *itself* as a partner working with the others in education/ outreach provision, or even as the leading node of such a partnership. Instead it behaved like a struggling arts centre trying to improve cash flow on its own. The core partners were treated poorly. Facilities were inadequate – the seating arrangements made the Circus 2 studio theatre space far less flexible than many of its potential users had assumed, and there were continual problems with heating and cleaning. Arrangements were often changed at the last minute to accommodate casual fee-paying incomers, displacing those expected to have spaces they had booked for teaching, thus disrupting NewVIc's education provision, and other partnership activities.

Nonetheless, all those consulted – including representatives of all the core partners – agreed that the Circus was in many ways good for their projects. One respondent went so far as to say 'being here has been great for us'. By late 2002, respondents were agreed that relationships between Circus management and core partners were improving, and so was the response to their demands. In this experiment in the collaborative operation of a complex venue through a complex trans-organisational partnership, there was no single Artistic Director and programming. Education work and commercial hires were subject to continuous – and occasionally heated – negotiation. And the relatively unstructured and unconstituted nature of the relationship continued.

The Salway Arts management controlled all the building's physical resources, including, for example, NewVIc-owned equipment kept in locked cupboards to which NewVIc staff did not have keys or codes. The office space for NewVIc staff was wholly inadequate. Even NewVIc's creative industries manager, whose day-to-day responsibilities include the management of Circus Media, shared hot-desking facilities in an open-plan office, and had no personal space, though some core partners did have better facilities in the Circus building.

By Spring 2002, both Salway Arts and the Theatre Royal Stratford East (TRSE) had admitted serious financial difficulty, with substantial operating deficits forecast. Following the departure of the founding Director, and the rapid turnover of Salway Arts staff, a part-time acting Chief Executive was appointed. Salway Arts and TRSE were admitted to Arts Council England's 'stabilisation and recovery'[22] programme in June 2002. Both Newham Council and Arts Council England provided further funding, and consultants were appointed to advise on the Circus's future, but in August 2003 the relationship with Salway Arts was terminated, and the Circus's doors were, albeit briefly and symbolically, closed. Salway Arts went into voluntary liquidation and administrators were appointed.

Several rounds of discussion followed, involving Arts Council England (London), Newham Council, NewVIc and the other core partners. Arts Council England had apparently again delivered a large sum of Lottery funding without securing a charge over the building. Yet the Arts Council still felt justified in leading the discussions about the future of a building over which it had no legal charge and for which it was by then providing no funding, and it was allowed to proceed on that basis. Three ACE Regularly Funded Organisations – Theatre Venture, East London Dance and Urban Development – were resident in the building, all with their own funding officers and separate revenue streams, but with no overall subsidy for running the building itself forthcoming from ACE. The complexity and intricacy of the partnership arrangements created a situation in which communicating vision and strategy to the multiple and overlapping funders and stakeholders became challenging, not least for Newham Council.

After the liquidation of Salway, Newham Council moved quickly to ensure that the building remained open for the programmes of the resident organisations while a longer term solution was sought. Intensive negotiations and the construction of a new business plan followed. It was proposed that control of the building would pass to NewVIc as lead organisation in the consortium.[23] The business plan, collaboratively drawn up between the resident organisations, provided for NewVIc to take on interim management of the building while options could be explored for developing a new trust or holding company.

Achievement of excellence in partnership

This is not a study in failure. Despite the commercial and operational troubles, the Circus had from the start been home to some excellent work in education and community arts such as that evaluated here as part of the *Pathways into Creativity* project. In this module from the UEL/NewVIc HND in performing arts in the community, students moved through the whole process of researching, devising and performing new drama. The project applied approaches to teaching and learning which resonate with the case studies described in Chapters 3 and 4.

This was the third cohort of the HND. The group was almost aggressively inclusive: it included people who used wheelchairs, people who appeared to have learning difficulties, people with communication problems, and an ethnic mix fairly typical of the area. What emerged was an exemplary higher education performing arts experience.

In devising their piece, the students worked with playwright Carl Reid, himself a course graduate and social worker, and three NewVIc staff: drama teacher Andy Cobb, choreographer and dance teacher Jo Parkes and theatre designer Jackie Sands. Carl Reid had wanted to learn about acting on order to write and this was his second collaboration with NewVIc HND students. His *Hair Pieces* had been a success the year before, and he did a third show in 2004. After three sessions of research, discussion and devising, Carl started writing a draft for a first rehearsal session. The script was twice redrafted and by the beginning of May Carl, in his words, 'let go' and Andy and Jo led intensive rehearsal for the late May show.

Schlat – an impact title – was about institutionalisation, imprisonment, exclusion and inclusion, and especially the institutionalisation-track of young offenders from children's home to prison. Despite the gloomy subject matter, Carl Reid's original ideas used a wide range of techniques and various kinds of comedy. The richness of Carl's creation was splendidly realised in the final performance – one highlight being a duet by Dennis-Potteresque magistrates singing in Jamaican patois.

The first devising session observed ran from 11am to 12.30. After lunch, students attended a talk and question-and-answer session about the experience of working with prisoners, given by a member of NewVIc staff who had done education work in prisons. Research by the group had also included talking with film director Mike Leigh, and taking observation walks – for example to observe the policing of black neighbourhoods.

For the first observed session students were asked to prepare a monologue and bring a prop. The group, led but not dominated by Carl and Andy, began by discussing the institutionalisation and nature of power relationships. They debated fixed behaviour and the possibilities of transformation. While they introduced their monologues and props, the students swapped news-based and personal anecdotes about power, control and social work. Some of them are social workers, others clients or former clients of social workers. One French student with partial hearing, who has a translator/assistant, discussed the recent British gangster-movie culture and its effect on heightening awareness and moral panic about criminality. He drew on Foucault to explain his ideas about institutionalisation and power, considering the uses of medication as well as prison.[24] Other students remarked on in-prison bravado and the role of prison as a home for some people, or as 'an addiction'. They talked about how asylum seekers can be victims of the prison system. They discussed the need in the drama itself to find some positive spin. The monologues were all about an aspect of victimhood, although one student used the examples of Nelson Mandela and Malcolm X to illustrate how imprisonment can be used positively. Each student delivered their prepared monologue and then talked about it and invited colleagues and teachers to comment.

In the second observed session a week later, students read through the first draft of Carl's script with Andy and Jo. Carl said he had written angrily, though he had obviously incorporated themes raised in the previous week's presentations and discussions. Later there was a second reading of the first draft of the first act. Students were asked to provide more feedback for Carl, to clarify characterisation, think about potential staging, and to read interactively – which on the whole they did not, although they did ask relevant questions and join in the envisioning of the staging. Brechtian alienation was mentioned a few times, and initial thoughts expressed about light and sound. There was some discussion of the representation of bad characters – they compared the difficulty this presented to them as actors with that of kissing on stage, and agreed that they would have to 'go for it' even if they play nasty characters. This discussion on the realisation of the ideas in the script also raised the issue of the 'adult' nature of the performance – as well as 'bad' language the script depicted murder, self-harm, and some nudity in a strip-search scene. So it would be unsuitable to put on at NewVIc, but could be presented at Stratford Circus, probably billed as an adults-only show. This meant NewVIc pupils under 18 could not see it.

The students read seated in a circle, helped and encouraged by their colleagues and the staff. Then, after a vocal and physical warmup led by a student, they broke into three groups, exploiting the large space. Each group worked on one surreal and one realistic scene for 20 minutes with a little staff help and advice, then presented the results to each other, this time using the performance space more actively. After feedback and discussion about the performances, free West End theatre tickets were given out. The students are encouraged to observe professional practice throughout the course.

The show attracted good houses. It was in two acts and used video information to support the onstage action, with an intriguing mix of surreal, comic and realist representations of the bleakness of institutional life. By the time of the observed performance it had run twice, and was apparently altered after each one. Some participants spoke of 'censorship' – though it was obviously self-imposed or mutually agreed – to describe the various cuts in both words and actions after the first performance.

The students were active learners at all stages of the project, and enjoyed

■ making input into early drafts of script

■ the open discussions of problems of performance

■ not just performing but being involved in design, marketing, sound and light design, front of house, etc

■ working with the course graduate as script writer. Carl was a role model to them all

■ working in Stratford Circus, a professional, non-school environment

■ an ultimate product that was funny, entertaining and inclusive of performers with a wide range of abilities, while also communicating the seriousness of the issues raised

A reception was held after the final performance and this gave participants a chance to interact with the audience. Everyone involved, and those consulted during its development or after they had seen the show – teaching and administrative staff and students – agreed that the Stratford Circus building had hugely contributed to this educational excellence. Students liked it precisely because it did not feel like college.

Remodelling the idea of a cultural quarter

The Circus offered more than qualifications-based education. It offered opportunities to engage with the community. Circus Media[25], an initiative led by NewVIc and housed in the Circus building, provides advice and technical facilities for local cultural-industry business startups. It had over 100 clients on its books at the time of the study, most of them young people from a range of ethnic groups, and a number of innovative projects.

The pioneering arts in health programme developed during 2002-3 under the education programme of Stratford Circus has the potential to transform the quality of life of people in the wider community. It works across the partnership, involving artists, tutors and workshop leaders contracted through East London Dance, Theatre Venture and NEWCEYS, to develop projects in a variety of settings including local hospitals and community centres. East London Dance has partnered with NewVIc to draw funding to develop a part-time adult education programme, the Community Dance Practitioner. Again with NewVIc staff, they created a nationwide training programme in integrated and inclusive dance practice, People Moving. And Theatre Venture had worked with NewVIc to develop a media skills training programme, Fast Forward to Media, for local unemployed adults. Summer school projects, choreographic workshops, events in collaboration with media organisations and a steady stream of visiting companies and artists all contribute to the mix.

Music business seminars are held at Stratford Circus each year in conjunction with Circus Media and Urban Development. Industry experts make their expertise available to anyone who registers for informal evening discussions and networking opportunities. This series draws in local people who are usually not looking for educational qualifications but are glad to learn from the seminars. If the cultural quarter is to exist as more than a place for business start-up and/or professional performance, informal educational opportunities of this kind must be nurtured. They are a valuable part of lifelong learning, in direct relationship to the employment potential of the creative industries. A position paper written in 2004 by the partners of the cultural quarter noted:

> A high proportion of creative industries workers are self-employed. One strategy for ensuing high quality prospects for the local community within the creative industries sector rather than just the lower level service jobs is to target communities in areas where there is a rapidly increasing creative industries sector with programmes of business support. In east London there is a high level of local aspiration to set up creative industries SMEs and the Circus Media programme is a response to both opportunities and barriers within the creative industries for people living in east London. These include: the lack of clear pathways into employment in the creative sector[26]; new markets that will be created by major regeneration and development in east London[27] which present new opportunities for the creative industries to contribute directly to regeneration and to provide products and services to new customers, but are also likely to fuel gentrification and exclusion (see Blake and Jeffery, 2001a; Attfield, 1999 and DCMS, 2004); and technological innovation and digitisation: consumer end equipment can be used to make and distribute high quality work which can be distributed rapidly locally, regionally and internationally.

A success story?

A report on *Hair Pieces* in mid-2003 made a prophetic point:

> In particular the 'ecology' of the relationships and networks around Stratford Cultural Quarter ... provides for a rich mix of opportunities for collaboration – but this ecology needs to be carefully tended in order for maximum benefits to be obtained.[28]

If Stratford Circus is seen as a partnership between a number of organisations that offer specific performance, educational and outreach experiences, it could be a jewel in the crown in the cultural development of the Thames Gateway, a model for future developments of international relevance. This model would replicate, for the creative industries and for artistic exploration, the science-park model of education-to-work which has benefited certain UK universities, notably Cambridge but also UEL, and also the national economy. Such a working model would support the continuing investment in the arts as educational tools for those wishing to work in the creative industries.[29] Given the right strategic planning and funding impetus the Circus could be at once a key provider of useful education to a diverse local community, an exciting performing arts space, and a creative industries hub. Building on models such as the Arc and the Sage, and on the successes of the Circus so far, the workings of the cultural quarter could be conceptualised in a new and exciting way. It would involve linear provision of work with schools, progress through further and higher education and lead ultimately to business start-up.

As the new lessees of the Circus, NewVIc and its collaborating organisations is placed to build on its achievements so far and realise such possibilities. But as one correspondent observed:

> Extraordinary leadership will be needed. What will make or break the project will be whether everyone develops real and honest commitment to shared leadership and shared responsibility, and that includes the people at the top as well as those at the bottom of the organisations.

Will the broader political, strategic and organisational backing required be forthcoming from the funders and organisations? And will the managers and gatekeepers support the interlocking relationships on which this model depends? Will such a risky, complex and groundbreaking model that could offer so much to so many be allowed to take root?

Notes

1   The assessment used the following methods. The literature on arts administration, education and regeneration in the performing arts was reviewed. Preliminary meetings involved academic and administrative staff from NewVIc, and the other core partners involved in the delivery of education and outreach programmes at Stratford Circus; most of these staff were later interviewed, as were staff from the Circus's resident organisations, the University of East London, Theatre Royal Stratford East, and Arts Council England. Past and present students were interviewed, and teaching sessions and student performances in both music and performing arts were observed, plus one of the outreach sessions conducted at Stratford Circus by Urban Development. I am very grateful to all who gave of their time. A brief report drafted in June 2003 was followed by two more versions. The November 2003 report provides the basis for this chapter.

2   See e.g. Gill Johnson *et al, New Audiences for the Arts*, Arts Council England, 2004; in particular the Council's Decibel programme, which aimed to encourage ethnic minority participation at all professional levels of creativity, performance and administration.

3   e.g. DCMS, *Culture at the Heart of Regeneration*, 2004, and its evidential precursor, Evans, G. and Shaw, P. *The Contribution of Culture to Regeneration. A Review of Evidence*, London Metropolitan University, 2004; DCMS, *Leading the Good Life. Guidance on Integrating Cultural and Community Strategies*, 2004; The British Academy, '*That full compliment of Riches*': the contribution of the arts, humanities and social sciences to the nation's wealth, 2004

4   Tessa Jowell, Secretary of State at DCMS, *Government and the Value of Culture* DCMS, 2004, among whose many rejoinders were J. Cowling, ed., *For Art's Sake? Society and the Arts in the 21st Century*, Institute for Public Policy Research, 2004.

5   Mayor of London, *London – Cultural Capital* consultative document, March 2003, executive summary, pp.16-17. The final strategy was published as *London Cultural Capital. Realising the Potential of a World-Class City*. Greater London Authority, 2004.

6   *London – Cultural Capital* pp16-17

7   *Ibid.,* pp17-18.

8   *Ibid.,* pp19-22

9   *Ibid.,* pp22-23

10 'Creative Journeys', the *Guardian* 24.6.2003, via www.Guardian.co.uk, accessed 24.6.03

11 www.nesta.org.uk , accessed 12.9.03.

12 National Audit Office, *Progress on 15 Major Capital projects Funded by Arts Council England,* HMSO, 2003, p7; see also House of Commons Committee of Public Accounts, *Progress on 15 Major Capital projects Funded by Arts Council England*, HMSO, 2004, pp4-5

13 A non-exhaustive list of other UK arts centre projects based on the 'mixed economy/ cross-sector partnership' principle, combining education-participation-regeneration-performanc, might also include: the refurbished De La Warr Pavilion in Bexhill-on-Sea (one of the original 'people's palaces'), the Rich Mix Centre under construction in Whitechapel, Artsdepot in Barnet, The Drum in Birmingham, C-PLEX in West Bromwich , The Junction in Cambridge, The Lowry in Salford, Dundee Contemporary Arts Centre, Baltic in Gateshead, etc.

14 *Ibid* pp11-12

15 www.arconline.co.uk accessed 12.08.04

16 see www.cafescientifique.org Most 'science' is currently, of course, an aspect of commercial research.

17 *News from Arts Council South East*, Arts Council 04.04., p.3

18 Press release, www.lda.gov.uk, 27/7/04, accessed 12.08.04

19 NewVIc Strategic Plan commentary: September 2001, 7th draft, p.4

20 G. Jeffery and P. McCormick, Newham Music Development Partnership, *Route Map* – discussion documents dated 30.4.2003 and 2.6.2003

21 At the time of this assessment, alongside NewVIc and its small-business-nurturing offshoot Circus Media, the core partners were, East London Dance, Theatre Venture, and NEWCEYS. Urban Development was by then a *de facto* core partner. Theatre Royal Stratford East as an original core partner became mired in its own financial and administrative problems and had become semi-detached from the venture, although both Stratford Circus and TRSE were being urged to collaborate more closely by ACE and LBN.

22 This programme provides assistance to arts organisations facing serious financial difficulties. At the time ACE had a client list of 40 organisations across the country.

23 A version of the Council's part in the Circus story, reported at its meeting of 17th August 2004, appeared at http://moderngov.newham.gov.uk/, (check ref) accessed 6.09.04

24 See for examples of this approach M. Foucault, The Birth of the Clinic (1973); *Discipline and Punish: the Birth of the Prison* (1977)

25 Circus Media is funded by the European Regional Development Fund Objective 2 programme and the London Development Agency.

26 This is confirmed by employers in the recent findings of the employer led research and development undertaken by Eminence Gris Ltd, commissioned by Thames Gateway Creative Skills Partnership – 'The power of word of mouth as a means of attracting applicants was acknowledged.' This presents specific barriers to people outside of networks and 'the present employment structure of the industry does not match the cultural diversity of the community where it is based' (Learning and Skills Council London East: Workforce development strategy for the cultural and creative industries)

27 The Olympic bid in the Lower Lea Valley, the Channel Tunnel Rail Link passenger terminus, Stratford City (the major redevelopment of Stratford's railway lands) and Thames Gateway (a package of development sites that will result in a city sub-region 'the size of Leeds')

28 'What Makes a Creative Partnership?' discussion paper for Pathways into Creativity and Animarts conference at Stratford Circus, 2.5.2003, p.3 (available on www.newvic-creative. org.uk)

29 Such examples provide a corrective to the bland assumptions contained in, for example, the *Music Manifesto*, released by the DfES in June 2004 to a blaze of publicity and ostensibly backed by key parts of the music industry – but with no initial commitment to increase funding of musical opportunities in secondary schools or elsewhere.

7

Leading creatively... creating leadership

Graham Jeffery

This chapter examines the implications of creative partnership for leadership and knowledge sharing. It draws on work in the US and Europe, and suggests further lines of enquiry for practitioners, researchers and policymakers to explore together.

Organisational hacking

Castells and Himanen (2002) describe the culture of innovation needed for survival and prosperity in the informational society as a 'hacker ethic'. Cultures of innovation require networks of collaboration, driven by the enthusiasm and energies of the hacker. 'Hackers want to realise themselves fully, to use their special creative capabilities, to constantly surpass themselves, and to produce creative work as a result of their actions' (2002, p46). Hackers work in networks to share ideas, developing new technologies and approaches which need to be modelled at multiple levels – within the work group, between organisations, and across sectors. 'At the national level, the growing significance of networking for innovation means that, for a country, the critical question is what kind of innovation network its public, private and citizen sectors form together' (Castells and Himanen, 2002, p48).

The work described in this book could be conceptualised as a form of organisational hacking. It comes from an 'activist' frame of mind. The team has taken and refined the core values of the college and developed new approaches to learning programmes which have moved students, staff and community participants beyond established boundaries. The shared spaces at Stratford Circus, the physical proximity of partners and the college's relatively sophisticated ICT systems have all helped.

The rhetoric of collaboration is everywhere, fed partly by the communicative possibilities of new technologies and telecommunications. And this fuels a competitive dynamic in which organisations seek 'collaborative advantage' (Huxham, 2000) in order to solve shared problems or develop new programmes of work. There *are* possibilities for rapid communication and sharing embedded in the new technologies, which enable simultaneous and a-synchronous communication to multiple audiences at different scales and through different media by means of what Mitchell (1999) describes as 'telepresence'. But – and this is an important issue for champions of e-learning and 'networked institutions' – telepresence, instantaneous communication and rapid response is reserved for people who have privileged access to informational networks. To take full advantage of the potential of e-learning, institutional structures and the working patterns of teachers lives will have to shift radically from conventional time-tabling and classroom based learning.

Developing effective collaborative learning programmes requires time for research and development, and for staff mobility. Huxham (2000) points out that partnership working is often posited on an untested hypothesis of 'collaborative advantage', which may ignore the high transaction costs and hidden labour costs required for sustaining collaboration and communication between organisations. Accounting has to allow for the time involved in partnership development and take a long-term view of its benefits or risks.

Given the pressures on learning institutions, partnership working can be difficult and painful for people on the front line. Mannie Sher pointed out in a presentation in October 2003 that the 'hidden life' of partnership involves unresolved tensions between the actors, which are at times based on the 'primitive drives' of resentment, power hunger, or exploitation. In contrast, the public face of partnership must convey unity of purpose and shared values. The process of resolving differences and reaching shared solutions, to achieve an ethical and honest public face means that trust has to be built between all the partners and they must learn to be reflective, self-critical and open to change. Such approaches sharply contrast with more common uses of the rhetoric of partnership, which can mask difference or hide the acquisition of resources. Behaviours modelled by individuals in partnership-building need to be mirrored in organisational forms. Questions of power relations can only be tackled if all the people involved are committed to listen and learn.

Building capacity for partnership working

The models of partnership described in this book have evolved from small beginnings. They come from a commitment to develop dialogical frameworks for learning in which conversations between learners, teachers and outside agencies enable the design of projects. They could entail building in work with a visiting artist in weekly lesson over three or four weeks, or taking students off timetable and off site for two or three days, or bringing more than one group, or two or three teachers, together. It helps that students have a sense of ownership due to the college's commitment to student welfare and mutual support. The approach has some features in common with the 'minischool' or 'flexischool' proposed in the late 1980s (see Toogood and Meighan, 1992).

Huxham and Vangen (2003) describe the process of partnership building in terms of a trust-building cycle:

- ■ Start small, have modest aims

- ■ Build trust and confidence

- ■ Review and evaluate

- ■ Develop more ambitious collaboration...

Provided it keeps revolving through positive feedback, this planning cycle helps to develop longer-term relationships. A partnership is often a stage on the road to new organisational forms[1] and should be understood as a kind of *emergent* organisational form. Partnership working means struggling with boundaries, problems of definition, and constantly evolving organisational roles. In partnership, the institution's organisational structures need to keep up with emergent relationships. This may precipitate problems of communication and managing information flows and decision making – horizontally, vertically, internally, externally. Conflicts and boundary problems are inevitable and constructive, provided everyone is willing to learn from them.[2]

If innovation takes place mainly at the edges and boundaries of organisations, they need to think about how they embed – or reject – those innovations in relation to their evolving systems. As a colleague recently said to me, models which have been developed primarily for a business context (e.g. Senge, 1990) in which the bottom line is generally clearly defined, do not necessarily transfer neatly to educational contexts where the educational bottom line is the subject of fierce contestation, where value systems are often more tacit and implicit, and where outcomes cannot be measured in simple financial or accounting terms.

Redistributive leadership

Recent research on models of leadership and management for a knowledge society has focused on the notion of distributed, distributive, or dispersed leadership.

> The increasing role of values, communication and interpersonal relationships, and the central importance of responding to, and shaping continuous change challenge all those in leadership positions... There is growing recognition that good leadership needs to be understood as a systematic process which is distributed across whole organisations, and represented in the relationships between leaders and followers at all levels, rather than just concentrated in the behaviour of those in the most senior leadership position. (Horne and Jones, 2002, p1)

The characteristics of education organisations with dispersed leadership would incorporate numerous shared spaces – teachers collaborating internally and externally, learners working independently, shared offices, shared classrooms, sharing resources beyond the institution. Boundaries are still maintained but are seen as not fixed but permeable and flexible.

As part of the research for this chapter I had long conversations by email and in person with Sonia Khan, NewVIc's Creative Industries Development Manager from 2002 to 2004. She agreed for some of this to be reproduced below, because she is so clear about the difficulties and tensions in partnership working.

I asked Sonia what she felt that the notion of redistributive leadership meant. The team had begun to use this term, to see if it described the way that we were thinking about leadership – an attempt to construct a variant of 'distributed leadership' that emphasised the active and conscious redistribution and sharing of power by those in leadership positions. Redistributive leadership meant to her:

> The opposite of the traditional management model in education, which seems to mimic the traditional classroom dynamic with teachers as 'receivers' of decisions rather than co-producers of decision-making. Key features should be:

- sharing information to empower people to participate in decision making

- cycles of review, evaluation and forward planning

- collective plans and objectives that guide, inform and authorise decision making – so that decisions aren't made under duress or at the eleventh hour

- taking people out of their comfort zone – so that no-one feels there is a 'force' who will make all the decisions for them

- making everyone in a team feel that their ideas count and that their role is vital

- enabling management and collaborative decision making – moving beyond rhetoric and into a real commitment to dialogue (Email, 20 September 2004)

Secondly, we talked about how we could move beyond pockets of innovation in arts learning and embed a culture of creativity more broadly in the college as a whole. We discussed some of the specific features of arts-based learning processes at NewVIc and why teachers and practitioners of the arts may be more enthusiastic than others about partnerships and open-ended approaches to learning. Was there something about arts-based learning cultures that leant itself more readily to collaborative working; and was one inhibitor of creativity for teachers of non-arts subjects that they didn't see their work in such expansive terms?

Sonia observed that the problem is that educational institutions, driven hard by audit cultures, are often based on 'a culture of achievement based on conformity with the norm rather than challenge and creativity = a culture dominated by petty bureaucrats and gatekeepers = disempowered unhappy employees = people who try to do as little as possible!'

This creates a vicious circle:

> In such a culture, when there is an attempt to widen the power base, conformists are more likely to be attracted to and to succeed in accessing the management positions. They will not be the right people to challenge the systems and so will be ineffective decision makers. The bottle-neck in decision making which they were meant to help alleviate is not widened.

I asked whether she thought the idea of reciprocity or shared partnership was clearly understood in the college, and she replied:

> There is an old guard view in education that partnerships are merely vehicles for securing funding or making decisions collectively. Many

organisational cultures in education are very monolithic and introspective so the idea of partnership is not part of the core ethos understood by all employees, despite the rhetoric of mission statements and the isolated pockets of interest at senior management/middle management and team level.

This echoes the issues discussed in Chapter 5. Is it possible, or even desirable, for large scale public sector institutions, which have to respond to many contradictory and turbulent drivers, to develop a consistently innovative and inclusive partnership-based learning culture?

Definitions of partnership – and questions of power

New Labour's mantra of partnership implies *reciprocity*: mutual self-help and exchange (Glendinning *et al*, 2002). Partnership is not defined as a simple supplier-customer or principal-agent relationship. A huge range of models of partnership operate even within our single institution – from verbal commitments and back of envelope contact to tightly worded, furiously argued legal agreements, protocols and memoranda of co-operation.

Sonia Khan commented in an email that:

If you look at what is happening across the publicly funded sector, it's easy to envisage that in time public institutions will all be 'enablers' and 'facilitators' engaged in networked delivery of learning/health/local services rather than direct deliverers in order to ensure greater flexibility and innovation.

As a form of emergent organisation, 'networked delivery' requires some clear models. Sonia suggested three contrasting typologies of partnership, and the need to understand where in the landscape each fits:

■ strategic partnership – sharing information and planning together but not doing

■ delivery partnerships – with a single institution as lead

■ joint ventures – parity of all partners

If I was going to draw an image to describe these different models I could say the strategic is a joining the dots, the delivery partnership is a hub and spokes and the joint venture is a daisy chain. And all partnerships that exist need to be embedded with written agreements, to avoid confusion or the more powerful partner moving the goalposts.[3]

Research by Huxham (2000, 2003), the UK Government's Public Services Productivity Panel (2002) and Doyle (2004) all repeatedly emphasises the need for greater clarity of definition, purpose and process within partnership working. All these studies challenge vague claims of 'mutual benefit', pointing to the need for analysis and critical awareness of the internal dilemmas and complex power relations involved in partnership working.

Developing a relationship with an outside provider increases resources and may give learners access to extended networks, which should lead to greater opportunities for progression, mobility and eventual employment. But to sustain it this relationship must be based upon both softer 'structures of feeling' and harder systems and procedures, and on a commitment to negotiation of differences and power sharing. Huxham's sophisticated analysis of the dynamics of collaborative working points above all to the understanding that conflicts and collisions – of values, of explicit and implicit intentions, of stated purpose versus hidden purpose – are an inevitable feature of sustained partnership.

If the educational partner is well resourced in terms of financial capital but concerned only superficially about equality or reciprocity, relationships may be tilted towards incorporation, not partnership. At worst, partnership may become a euphemism for domination, exploitation or colonisation. As Sonia remarked: 'the devil is in the detail: attention to processes and procedures is important because that's the stuff of relationship building. A rhetoric of collaboration without the means to activate it won't work' (interview transcript, 2004).

Johnstone (2003), drawing on research from Tuckman (1965), describes the stages of partnership development, as: 1. formation; 2. frustration; 3. function (or fail); 4. fly (or fail!) He suggests that many partnerships have some 'common needs' within the critical 'third stage' of their life cycle which include:

- focusing... minds on a powerful vision and mission for the partnership, with a clear statement of the added value that the partnership will deliver
- improving the quality of data about needs which partners seek to address
- using the power of evidence to encourage partners to consider learner/ community needs rather than their vested interests
- leaders in partner organisations creating supportive conditions and delegating authority for partnership within their organisations...
- clarifying partner roles, responsibilities and the advantage they gain from their commitment to the partnership. (Johnstone, 2003, p15)

Creative partnership needs to be underpinned by systems of management and communication. Sonia made the case that systems and creativity should not be regarded as in immutable opposition.

> We've got to challenge the idea that there is only room for the maverick genius as a leader who leaves the detail to the grey systems people. Ironically teachers need to combine these skills in the classroom in order to deliver the curriculum but are often discouraged from being multidisciplinary outside of the classroom. I think this will be difficult to shift in the arts and education worlds because they are both are based on traditionally hierarchical organisations that separate admin from delivery but the following might help:
>
> ■ Looking for people who can combine innovation and creativity with a methodical and systematic approach
>
> ■ Applying greater parity between systems and creativity
>
> ■ Designing bespoke systems that are appropriate for the work
>
> ■ Summarising the external requirements of work such as funders' requirements so that everyone understands them. (Email, 20 September 2004)

The innovation cycle: how to avoid boom and bust

An organisation that encourages devolved decision-making needs to be able to learn from the consequences of this approach. Organisational systems and job roles are unlikely to keep pace with change and innovation. In rapidly evolving organisations time needs to be set aside for review, adjustment and adaptation. As von Stamm (2003a, p386-387) points out, restriction and constraint does not necessarily strangle innovation. An essential feature of an innovative culture is an ability to learn from failure and to narrow down innovative ideas to those which are useful and relevant to the core purposes and mission of the organisation.

Accountability and quality systems tend to act as a brake on innovation. They require explanations, rationales, advocacy and clear communication from the team undertaking the innovation. The dynamic between originating new ideas and embedding innovation in order to change institutional practices is a cycle (see opposite).

ACCOUNTABILITY

An institution or education system's way of keeping track of what people are doing and why they are doing it, sometimes used in gatekeeper management as a blunt instrument to suppress or discourage innovation

EMBEDDING	**INNOVATION**
• advocacy	• development of ideas
• upwards/downwards/sideways communication	• devolved decisions
	• appropriate risk-taking
• navigating and using (and sometimes feeling abused by) quality assurance systems	• individual hunches
	• flexibility/openness to change
• evaluation methods	
• assessment	• evolution, shifting roles
• strategic thinking	• finding ways round blockages
• embedding change in systems	• operational, often crisis management
	• exploring and testing hypotheses

SUPPORT

Support is only genuine if people are honest with each other: the word support is often used in education for what is really domination

Models of professional development
Building on the multiplicity of teachers' roles, interests and experiences

This book positions the teacher as lead learner. She demonstrates her curiosity about how others learn and her own learning, and she feeds students' learning with her own interests and enthusiasms. In lampooning the twin ideologies of rock music's claim to artistic freedom of expression and the notion of school as a place of academic rules and regulation, Richard Linklater's film *School of Rock* (2003) makes a serious point. Curriculum 'breadth' can be achieved *through* depth, and through media with which students can engage when developing creative work. Learning through different intelligences – linguistic, logical-mathematical, musical and so on can be situated within project-based learning. The ironic twist to the film is that the kids and the anarchic artist-teacher who have become liberated through rock music end up with their musical activities relegated to after-school sessions, safely away from causing any more mayhem in the main-stream school curriculum.

In vocational learning, students work on problem-based tasks with physically evident and not just written outcomes. Different forms of knowledge – from technical skills to ideas realisation – can be integrated into problem-solving activity, including outcomes outside of the educational institution. This approach to learning involves a 'design' perspective on the curriculum (see Wenger, 1998). Students can use design processes to actively solve problems within their communities. We see this in recent work testing the Icelandic model of 'Innovation Education' in different European contexts (Gunnarsdottir, 2001), the Arts Council of England's Young People's Arts Award, and ASDAN's new Changemakers award for social enterprise in UK schools. These studies point to the powerful effects on young people of being offered freedom of choice, development of leadership skills and active physical engagement with materials and the learning environment.[4] They are supported by international evidence gathered by the Centre for Creative Communities (2004), and years of research by Shirley Brice Heath and colleagues (Brice Heath, 1998; Fiske, 1999) into the effects of situated, non-formal approaches to learning in community based youth arts organisations in the US and elsewhere.

Putting learning at the centre of project design

In a networked learning environment, teachers operate as cultural intermediaries at several levels. They interact with individual students and they facilitate groups. They work in curriculum development, represent the public face of the college, and negotiate inter-agency relationships. To thrive in networked learning systems and to build up partnership-rich institutions, teachers need training in these negotiating, project design and management skills. Skills of this kind are more familiar to creative professionals and artists, who are always developing new projects, products or services. Education is also a form of cultural industry (see Bourdieu, 1976a, 1976b) but many of its core organisational systems and learning paradigms remain little changed from the industrial institutional models of the late 19th and early 20th Century. In developing new models of critical vocational learning which aim to help students to make the transition to adopting professional values, and skills through partnership working, the college takes on a role as a cultural producer. Does this blurring of the boundaries between the institution and the profession, between formal and informal learning, between instruction, apprenticeship and invention, enable the learners' thinking to shift beyond education as a form of simulated exercise?[5]

Learning as research and development

All educational institutions need to embrace the value of *learning*. And this requires time for research and development. Such investment is costly and for many organisations outside of higher education that are driven by externally imposed targets and audit cultures, research and development time seems fanciful. Schools, colleges and arts organisations struggle to find time and resources for initiatives which challenge comfortable and accepted definitions of their core purpose. And it takes entrepreneurial skills and lateral thinking to lever resources for growth. But the kinds of institutional alliances described in this book might assist schools and colleges without a well developed research culture to think about how to join forces with organisations in the community and voluntary sector, the arts and creative industries, funding and development agencies or universities to develop networked – and inclusive – models of knowledge exchange and innovation. Such models expand the worlds occupied by both learners and teachers, and build individual pathways for progression.

Wenger (1998, p241) distinguishes between an unwritten 'community of practice' – what people actually do and how they behave in their everyday execution of their work – and the 'authored' institutional framework – what the institution states it is doing in policies, procedures and publicity. Organisations are 'constellations of practices' (p 246), but people who wield more power in organisations, or whose jobs provide them with more time to think and implement their thinking organisationally can better contribute to debates, enforce particular ways of working, or ignore or suppress ideas of which they disapprove. But the positional authority of managers or leaders is reinforced or undermined by the level of trust and confidence they inspire in their followers.

Management, audit and control

In our frenetic climate of managerialist audit and control, many employees and teachers may try to operate as independently of the world of organisational management as they can. As Andy Hargreaves (1994) and Michael Fielding (1999b) have identified, many teachers find a contradiction between an enforced culture of managerialist control and performativity and having a voluntary humanistic and empathetic approach to learners. The idea of teacher-artist-activist is an attempt to re-frame a more humanistic and creative professional identity for teachers than the narrow and uncritical managerialist-performative model that seems to prevail. Teachers are resistant to managerialist and economically reductive cultures in their profession, so more empowering models of leadership might encourage innovation.

Moreover, as the Centre for Educational Research and Innovation of the OECD (2004) points out, there is a clash between two different 'epistemic cultures' in education: – that of measurement, audit and accountability, and a humanistic culture based on the notion of professional autonomy, dialogue and reflective practice. The universalising and colonising features of audit culture suggest that educational outcomes can be standardised nationally or internationally, measured objectively, and be subject to 'random controlled trial'. Yet many communities of professional practice, supported by socio-cultural educational research, insist that educational outcomes cannot be simplified down to units of achievement, to absolute values or to replicable, idealised models of 'best practice' which fit all settings. A way needs to be found between the culture of public accountability, audit, and quality control, and the culture of a socially produced dialogue between professional expertise, established and emergent knowledge.

Educational institutions are built on systems and structures – timetabling, curriculum planning, blocking, registers, and all the paraphernalia of student tracking and monitoring. These technologies of control and accounting regulate the learning, the hours staff are deployed, what resources are available and how students' progress is monitored and evaluated. What is crucial is who has the power to decide how the teachers and students occupy time and space, and why. In their work, teachers negotiate between institutional and qualifications systems and the learners they work with. In explicit ways in schools and more tacit ways in post-compulsory education, learners are strongly acculturated to ways of organisational thinking which offer varying degrees of flexibility in access to resources, and variable definitions of work and learning. In enforcing standards of discourse, demeanour and even dress, institutions may subtly exclude experiences beyond formal classroom settings. Enforced standards determine what behaviours and practices are permitted, sanctioned or rewarded.

Organisational hackers seeking to innovate within such systems have to find ways of modifying or circumnavigating these largely invisible structures. But first one has to understand them, obtain a measure of ownership and control over them, and if evidence shows that as a result of change learners are more engaged and achieve high quality outcomes, be prepared to argue for systemic modifications.

Viral innovation and learning communities

Notions of the 'networked learning community' and 'viral innovation' (see e.g D. Hargreaves, 2003) inform recent thinking about reform of the UK education system. For knowledge acquisition and exchange to be sustainable they must be built into everyday work patterns. Teachers' daily working lives will need to change so they can communicate better laterally and externally. Imposing the rhetoric of the 'learning community' on exhausted schools (Gatto, 2002) and exhausted practitioners will only heighten stress levels, unless the institution adapts to working in a more networked and open way.

Hargreaves avers that the status of professionals who share their work and use networks and agencies to promote innovation needs to be raised. The altruistic forces that so powerfully shape teachers' professional identities, he argues, are precisely why schools and colleges should share their best practices. In a distributed learning network based on open-source principles, there would be commitment to sharing information, pooling resources and designing learning experiences collaboratively.

But it is unclear how the different forms of intra-institutional competition affect the capacity for innovation and knowledge exchange within the education system. The dynamic of competition brought about by marketised funding models for students, teaching and research may inhibit collaboration between institutions in the same sector.

Institutions need innovation; they need to develop their staff and they need 'best practices' in learning so as to maintain a competitive edge and adapt provision to the changing landscape of qualifications, employment and progression. One response is to seek collaborative advantage in clustering and networking, in sharing between professional communities. Since 1997, agencies such as the National College for School Leadership and the Higher Education Academy have advocated peer review, sharing 'good practice', and peer mentoring as central to strategies to improve and develop leadership capacity in public education.

But institutions increasingly have to compete for the most able students and the most capable teachers – and in HE, researchers – in order to maintain or improve their positions in crude league tables. This pseudo-market is inhospitable to openness and sharing: why should schools and colleges let go of their most valuable assets, and who pays for the time spent in collaborating and networking?

The focus on performance as measured in qualifications and test-score league tables also inhibits staff in schools and colleges from thinking more broadly about educational purpose, and leaves little space for innovation. The volume of content required to be taught by a heavily assessed quali-fications system is inimical to open and project-driven forms of learning in schools, except at the margins of the school day. As Sonia Khan noted, a climate of performativity is likely to create a risk-averse management culture in which teachers retreat into standardised and normative versions of teaching and learning. With a more open model of curriculum, teachers could develop relationships between different areas of study through pro-jects and develop investigatory and arts-based learning processes. Work in schools and colleges could become directly linked to community engage-ment and regeneration processes[6]. The Tomlinson proposals (2004) for reform of the 14-19 curriculum in the UK open up some such opportunities.

Added to this mix of push-pull factors is the policy drive to widen participa-tion and develop inclusive models of learning. Responses to this agenda have varied wildly between different institutions even within the same sector. In the UK, selective schools and elite universities have responded very differently to the challenges of inclusion. Their meritocratic approach seeks to select out the most gifted and talented students regardless of back-ground. It is proposed that scholarships, access funds and other incentives will mitigate the effect of variable tuition fees on access and participation. The former polytechnics, the further education sector, and schools with a commitment to comprehensive enrolment policies have turned to models of 'collegial entrepreneurship' (Clark, 2004, p7; Brighouse, 2002) as a means to re-frame their work and develop new modes of inclusion and knowledge transfer in the competitive and unequally funded marketplace.

There may be severe value clashes between the *modus operandi* of volun-tary and community sector organisations, whose prime purpose is to act as advocates and service providers for marginalised and excluded com-munities, and learning institutions, even though they profess the same aims of widening participation. The latter are driven by different values and priorities – by regional, national and international knowledge and qualifications markets, established academic discourses and hierarchies. They value quite different 'cultural capital'. In partnership working between the formal and the voluntary education sector, these tensions cause struggles over the form and content of the curriculum, modes of learning and knowledge reproduction, and the character of the social relationships that shape the participation of communities, learners and teachers in their institutions. Yet these struggles could be seen as a catalyst for shared learning.

People from different parts of these institutional worlds who want to work together have to negotiate between different epistemic and ethical cultures – scientific, medical, humanistic, academic, vocational (see OECD, 2004, and Apple, 2000). How can these epistemic cultures be reconfigured to form meaningful pathways for progression for those whose stories, cultures and traditions have been systematically excluded from learning institutions and the official national curricula (see Kearney, 2003)?

One governmental push towards innovation in the UK – and, arguably, democratisation – of learning and curricula is to penalise institutions financially which recruit students but do not retain them. Institutions, particularly those like NewVIc which have high numbers of non-traditional or disadvantaged students, may need to review their modes of teaching, learning and pastoral support to ensure the success of their students. But since inclusion is not rewarded nearly as handsomely as excellence, and the two are frequently seen as in opposition, some institutions may become more rather than less selective, in the fear that students seen as risky will adversely affect league-table and funding positions.

The professed democratisation of widening participation has led to heated debate about dumbing down and the worth of mass participation in further and higher education (Wolf, 2002; Deer, 2003). Institutions serving affluent communities have traditionally defined high achieving intakes. So they are less likely to be penalised and need to become more inclusive, or share their innovations.

As personalised learning moves to the centre of education policy, will 'personalisation' be about further embedding radical individualism and the ideologies of the market such as freedom of choice in public institutions? Or can it be about person-centred learning, built in relation to the multiple social and cultural histories that constitute the self? The ideology of the 'autonomous self': a-social, a-cultural, a-political, is still a core social and economic driver. As David Harvey (2000, p236) says about public culture in the US:

Private property and inheritance, market exchange, commodification and monetisation, the organisation of economic security and social power, all place a premium upon personalised private property vested in the self (understood as a bounded entity, a non-porous individual) as well as in house, land, money, means of production, etc., all construed as the elemental socio-temporal forms of political-economic life.

This book has suggested some alternative ways of thinking. Our models of person centred learning challenge the powerfully normative, homogenising and standardising approaches to learning promoted by market ideologies. They try to harness the discourses of 'creativity' and 'entrepreneurship' into a critical framework for inclusive and effective education.

A blend of non-formal, informal, and formal learning

Writing about the role of young peoples' learning in informal and community settings, Shirley Brice Heath, (2004) says this:

To define 'outcomes' or 'achievement' narrowly and primarily in terms of school achievement is to risk loss of the learning power that carries creativity into functional and critical uses that sustain and expand human capital. (2004: p1)

Within the NewVIc learning culture, the opportunities to mix formal and informal learning provides a 'blended' environment which values individual aspirations and interests, and affirms diversity. The arts and media team have always sought to give students access to resources outside of timetabled classes to do their own thing as well as college things; sensitivity to the rights of individuals to self-expression is evident. A student who is now a successful producer/rapper in East London's underground hip-hop scene, told us: 'it's because they encourage you to do what you can do and give you access to equipment – then you respect them more because they let you do your thing' (notes from discussion, 2003).

Music education has endorsed the value of informal and non-formal learning in developing cultures of achievement through the *Music Manifesto* (DFES, 2004b) and the Paul Hamlyn Foundation's *Musical Futures* research. Out of school hours or extra-curricular learning is increasingly recognised on both sides of the Atlantic as significant for developing students' sense of self-worth and inculcating a culture which values education. But anything that is seen as additional or optional will always have lower status than subjects delivered in the timetabled formal curriculum. This makes non-formal learning much more vulnerable to funding cuts and short-termism.

I argue for a much more radical approach to the design of learning institutions. Formal and informal learning cultures need to be woven together more tightly, and learners offered real choices and responsibility. The arts curriculum should be more situated and project-based and should integrate theoretical and critical enquiry in a problem-solving praxis. Within such learning centres, youth and community arts organisations, many of them led by young people themselves, would assume a prominent role. As policy moves towards extended schools, as creativity moves out of the margins of educational thinking, and as community education undergoes something of a revival, this is a key area for investigation.

Timetables at NewVIc allocate staff time for additional or enhancement learning. Leading non-accredited and informal learning such as choirs, sport, clubs and activities is timetabled in the same way as classes leading to qualifications. We avoid the burnout that happens in schools which allow little time or space to enter collaborative relationships based on artistic or creative passions, except outside the formal timetable.

The development of higher education programmes has bought staff time for research and development. The university's semester system is run inside the further education college year, giving staff timetabled for higher education teaching some remission from the standard 22 hours per week contact-time college model. Although the staff are contracted to work the same hours as their colleagues, the HE semesters are ten weeks shorter than the FE year. This allows time for the research, preparation, curriculum development and trans-organisational administration associated with the HE teaching.

A constant theme that came out of our research and discussions with colleagues, students, parents, and community and industry partners was the notion of working across boundaries. Brokering learning across boundaries creates intrinsic and stealthy forms of professional development. The models of collaborative and team learning which enable the realisation of creative ambitions are highly motivating.

Etienne Wenger writes:

> Boundaries are important locations, but not just because they can cause problems. Discontinuities can be as productive as continuities for the negotiation of meaning. Boundaries are like fault lines: they are the locus of volcanic activity. They allow movement, they release tension; they create new mountains; they shake existing structures.
>
> ...they are a learning resource in their own right

...they are the likely locus of the production of radically new knowledge... where the unexpected can be expected, where innovative or unorthodox solutions can be found... also places where new practices often start. (1998, p254-5)

Creating leadership

The partnership-led model of further education, higher education and business support described in these pages could be seen as a prototype of integrated and inclusive progression for arts-based learning and creative industries development. At its core is the flexibility for learners to choose their own routes through the matrix of opportunities opened up by the partnership-based curriculum. The possible exit and entry points are numerous and if the system is flexible, learners can build their own opportunities. Certain community led enterprises from the United States provide other examples:

Little Black Pearl Workshop, Chicago

Led by and focused upon the local African American community, this provides training, development and in-school programmes in art and furniture design targeted particularly at young people labelled as 'at risk'. The products are sold and the profits reinvested in the organisation. It has successfully incubated many new businesses and in autumn 2004 moved into purpose built premises with workshop spaces, a large retail unit, a cafe and training and education space. It works in partnership with high schools, particularly on the extremely deprived South Side of Chicago.

In its after-school programmes for young people aged 10-19, participants learn to work with ceramic tiles, make furniture, and in the visual arts. They create products that are marketed and sold locally. Students are taught how to manage the whole process: purchasing supplies, securing a business license, marketing and negotiating contracts. They receive 20 per cent of the revenue from earned income.

> Many of the young people participating in LBPW's program live in public housing and come from families with little or no experience of the world of work. While LBPWs program focuses on youth, the generational character of poverty in its work with young people is also an avenue into families where adults are also in need of skills and connections to employment opportunities. (Ford Foundation, 2003, p24)

> Our program is based on art as a way of making a living. Our goal is to create avenues of self-sufficiency for the children in the neighbourhood who are most susceptible to ending up in prison. Foundations need to re-cognise our role in community development. Housing alone doesn't create a community.' Monica Haslip, Director (Ford Foundation, 2003, p47)

Artists for Humanity, Boston

Targeting African American and Latino young people living in the inner-city, this project has grown rapidly in the last ten years, developing young people as artists, leaders, entrepreneurs and creating work which engages with urban contexts and is exhibited across the city. Again, a shrewd business model ensures that the proceeds from products and services are reinvested in the enterprise. The young people who have worked within the organisation for some years are enabled to move into leadership and advocacy roles.

Further examples of such community based arts organisations in the US are documented in Shirley Brice Heath and Laura Smyth's: *ArtShow: youth arts and community development* (1999) and in the Ford Foundation's 2003 report, *Downside Up*.

Both of these examples have a bridging approach that supported routes into creative work and practical community regeneration. But would the tight identification of art and commerce in the organisations translate to a European context? The community arts movement has criticised the wholesale commodification of artistic practices and products.

However, many organisations in Newham are engaged in similar work. Colleagues at Waterhouse Studios, a community recording studio in Stratford, have developed models of mentoring and support for emerging artists, recently focusing on online applications and streaming audio. Urban Development (see Shaw, 2001), based at Stratford Circus, has established a new record label, supported by Black music industry professionals. It integrates a programme of education and outreach activity with promoting and mentoring professional and emerging artists in hip-hop and urban music forms. East London Dance has developed a new inclusive youth dance company. Theatre Venture runs a young actors' workshop at NewVIc.

The college's relationship with all these programmes indicates permeable boundaries between the identities of learners as students and the construction of their own pathways between their life-worlds and their work-worlds as artists, cultural workers or creative professionals. The critical issue is the next stage. Can programmes and projects be led by the participants themselves so that they move into positions of direct ownership and control over local cultural resources? This would develop 'leadership succession.'

Sasaki (2004) points out that ever since John Ruskin and William Morris the notion of cultural *work* rather than cultural *labour* is embedded in creative industry. This links to sociological and philosophical approaches to re-establish the concept of creative, as opposed to repetitive, work as having *ethical* roots, broader than employment solely for economic profit (see

Williams, 1959, p144-158). Such approaches recognise the value of work in honesty, respect and care for others, and offer a broader orientation towards social and ecological justice (see Fielding, 1999; Gardner *et al*, 2001; Orr, 2004). Attempts to construct the notion of community focused, ecological and dialogical aesthetics fit with these ideas (see for example Gablik, 1991; Kester, 2004). Talking to Ron Bieganski of Free Street Programs on a study visit to Chicago in spring 2003, I was struck by his insistence that he was treating the young people he worked with as artists. He told me:

> It's not therapy, it's not inclusion, it's not keeping them occupied or off the street, it's about them learning what it takes to be an artist, and how tough that is. We treat them as artists. (field note, 2003: see also Rashpal Singh Bansal's comments about his experience at NewVlc on page 35-36).

Chapter 5 explored the idea that some artists are special people because they can catalyse and re-frame the world in light of democratic and inclusive creativity. Our students are not expected to pursue a vision of the artist as 'isolated genius' or 'uniquely talented', or 'superstar'. Artists work across boundaries and at the intersection of communities and cultures, so they can be active agents in the reinvention of communities.

These principles are drawn in part from studies into 'asset-based community cultural development' (see Ford Foundation, 2003) and grassroots cultural organisations in the US. The cultural resources of communities in the US, with their ethnic and cultural diversity, are built on so that young people are regarded as assets in the regeneration and revitalisation of everyday life and economic development (see also Landry, 2000; Brice Heath and Robinson, 2004), and not criminalised or excluded as liabilities and risks[7]. Approaches to cultural and creative learning, linked explicitly to social and community regeneration have made only isolated inroads into the formal school or college curriculum in Western democracies.[8] Specialist critical theory and cultural studies discourses, and some postgraduate teaching within specialist departments of higher education, however, have focused on arts in context, arts and environment, socially engaged arts practices, or Joseph Beuys' concept of 'social sculpture'.

But such approaches largely remain on the outside of schools and further education, as grassroots enterprises in pioneering community and youth arts organisations.[9] Some of these organisations have begun to deliver out of school hours learning or summer schools; others have entered into validation partnerships with universities and colleges.[10] But for many such programmes integration into the core curriculum of schools and colleges remains problematic, often due to issues of control over time, space and resources. For example, Paul Teruel of Street-level Youth Media, another Chicago-based young people's media organisation, described how the organisation was expected by some schools with which they were working 'in partnership' to deliver 45 minute classes in 'video production' with thirty-plus students, with one video camera and one edit suite between them, which they had to provide themselves! Such inadequate approaches reveal the host institution's disregard for the knowledge and skills of the community partner.

The potential of schools to play a role in community regeneration and life-long learning is again attracting interest.[11] But as Helen Gould (2004) points out, there seems to be a general 'absence of cultural or creative thinking' in social policy. Approaches developed by Landry (2000) and Hawkes (2001) might help place community focused arts-based practices in education, re-generation and social inclusion higher on the UK's learning policy agenda. Recent work by UNESCO (2004) posits an entitlement to 'cultural rights' and seeks to find common indicators across societies of how participation in culture facilitates inclusion and social development.

These cultural policy and planning frameworks operate in the interstices of global, regional and local interests, and all are double-edged. The key ques-tion, to paraphrase Sharon Zukin (1995), is whose culture, whose policy, and whose plan is it? One country's cultural export is another's cultural im-port. So uncritically invoking the value and dynamism of creative industry in national economies within a neo-liberal discourse of business and enter-prise could suck arts and cultural activity deeper into neo-colonial and ex-clusionary processes.

Instead, clusters can be developed between arts and education organisa-tions and communities, such as described in this book. NewVIc teachers have reacted against the profound barriers, discrimination and prejudice faced by our students and their communities because of their ethnicity, gender, class and ability. We radically broadened the range of artists, re-sources, spaces and people we involved in our students' learning, and this helped them to make pathways for themselves into the cultural life of the city. We have gradually evolved mentoring cycles among ex-students and graduates, who become role models/learning support artists/visiting teachers and artists. Ex-NewVIc students have returned to the college as full time teachers. The voices of the college are now plural, the range of artistic and cultural practices more diverse.

The work in the Stratford Cultural Quarter aims to establish bottom-up eco-nomic and cultural development cycles to commission and support artistic work which reflects the communities that use the buildings. It will nourish new creative businesses and develop new cultural products and markets, keeping lifelong learning at its heart (see Chapter 6). The graduate status of our performing arts higher education programmes with UEL are enabling people from a far greater spread of backgrounds than a generation ago to enter teaching and cultural professions. The vision of a more diverse and inclusive education service and a democratised public culture can only be achieved through a long-term commitment to intervention and action.

The defining feature is an active and critical pedagogic approach that puts young people into positions of leadership and ownership. It is also about developing dialogical frameworks between institutions of learning and the communities they serve – what in the US is characterised as 'service learning' (Pearson, 2002). Dialogue is based upon an ethical understanding of public accountability rather than a functional and bureaucratic model. Ethical accountability would work as much sideways and downwards as upwards; as educators, their managers and their funders would seek to enter into dialogue with all the communities they serve.

Wenger (1998, p55-57) discusses learning in terms of 'trajectories of participation': 'Learning builds personal histories in relation to the histories of our communities – thus connecting our past and our future in a process of individual and collective becoming.' Creative partnership requires recognition of the intermediary role of the teacher and the artist between expertise and learning, between 'being' and 'becoming' within an ethics of dialogue, and recognition that this role is pivotal.

A few more questions
Instead of a conclusion, I offer some questions for further research and investigation:

It is time for teachers to conceptualise their identities around notions of activism, the 'hacker mentality', learning brokerage or design? What are the opportunities, risks and barriers to doing so?

Is it useful to frame creativity in post-14 learning as applied research and development, particularly in industrial or community contexts? How would this affect curriculum design and the organisation of courses?

What are the creativity paradigms that define modes of thinking, intelligence and knowledge creation in arts education?

How do the competing interests and demands of audit and accountability cultures, academic and vocational cultures, business and community cultures play out in extended and networked schools, colleges and universities?

Is there a greater role for a design[12] or brokerage perspective in teaching and learning?

How can we replace vague, unproven 'collaborative advantage' with precise partnership working in arts education?

Should a theory of cultural, symbolic and social capital[13] be applied to situated creativity and its social and cultural basis? Or does this mark the further subjugation of the academic and cultural field to the economic field (see Deer, 2003; Fine, 2000)? Should the notion of creative industry be accepted as the dominant paradigm for learning in the arts?

What would be the features of 'dialogical aesthetics' and 'dialogical ethics' (Kester, 1999) in an educational context?

To what extent does creativity discourse as currently practised in schools, colleges and universities facilitate a progressive and inclusive approach to issues of race, class, and gender? Or does it generally lead to 'containment, mastery and exploitation of cultural difference' (Sharma *et al*, 1996, p19)?

Is creativity discourse in danger of obscuring difference, conflict and contestation?

These are some of the many questions to address in our daily work through action and reflection. Our task as educators is not only to speak, write, instruct and to judge on grounds of authorship and authority. We also need to listen, think, respond, imagine, experiment, and be willing sometimes to fail.

Notes

1   An insight also from John Kelleher of the Tavistock Institute.

2   Florida (2002) identifies inbuilt tension between 'organisation' and creativity, and argues that industry is shifting from Fordist models of fixed, hierarchical organisational forms based on mechanistic models, to 'creative', post-industrial, networked and flexible modes of organisation. Other writers have developed models of educational management based on chaos/complexity theory, or systems theory. See, e.g. Caine, and Caine, 1997, Brooke-Smith, 2003.

3   Johnstone (2003) offers a typology of six different kinds of partnership: strategic alliance, joint venture, supply chain partnership, networking forums, advisory groups.

4   Brice Heath and Robinson, (2004, p118): 'Current work in evolutionary biology and the neurosciences increasingly examine the complexities of ways the young learn without verbal instruction... Social scientists are learning how youth actively engage in shaping and directing their own learning environments. Studies in the neurosciences and medically-informed theories of adolescent development, suggest that learning take place optimally during puberty and maturity toward adulthood through active movement, direct experience, and high-risk engaged-role learning.'

5   Such an approach might also call into question established modes of knowledge (re)production and the stratification of established and canonic forms of knowledge (see Apple, 2000; Deer, 2003; Strathern, 2000).

6   Crowther *et al* (2003, p43) put the dilemma like this. In the context of discussing the potential contribution of schools to area regeneration, 'this may mean reframing the question we ask of them. Instead of How can schools contribute to the regeneration of disadvantaged areas alongside their 'core business', we may need to ask: What is it about schools' core business that enhances the life-chances of all children in all communities that they serve (including those which experience disadvantage)?' As we pointed out in Chapter 2, an expansive interpretation of the college's mission is a key condition for a creative college.

7   Stanley Aronovitz, in Friere (1998: ppxxvi-xxvii): 'The relationship between the credentialled 'experts' of 'at risk' populations and the oppressed 'at risk' individuals has less to do with a democratic society than with a colonial society, although we are not allowed to call it so. If this colonial legacy remains unexamined and the 'at risk' students are denied the opportunity to study and critically understand their reality, including their language, culture, gender, ethnicity and class position, for all practical purposes the 'at risk' students will continue to experience a colonial existence. Instead of becoming enslaved by the management of the 'at risk' students, which enhances the economic interests of the 'at risk' functionaries, educators need to reconnect with our historical past so as to understand the colonial legacy that may undermine the democratic aspirations of 'at risk' programs.' Gale and Densmore (2000) also discuss 'deficit' models of educational achievement.

8   In England, Weekend Arts College, Second Wave Youth Arts, Inter-Action Trust, and Community Music, are early examples – and all began as 'voluntary' organisations. Some of the history of this work can be traced through the theatre-in-education movement (see Jackson, 1993) and the community arts movement (see for example Itzin, 1980; Coult and Kershaw, 1990; Everitt, 1997; Benjamin, 2002). In UK higher education, Dartington College of Arts probably has the longest pedigree in developing this way of thinking although more programmes in community and socially engaged arts springing are up all over the UK, and in the US. California State University at Monterey Bay, Columbia College, Chicago, and Hampshire College, Massacheusetts all have degree programmes which explicitly link together notions of inclusion, cultural production, social justice and community development. More examples from the HE and FE context internationally can be found at www.communityarts.net. UK organisation Creative Exchange maintains a database of international arts organisations working in the field of culture and development (www.creativeexchange.org.uk)

9   For some international examples in the anglophone world of work in youth arts and community development, see Eames, 2003; Putnam and Feldstein, 2003; Kester, 2004; and Rabkin and Redmond, 2004. For examples from the UK, see Ings, 2002; British Council, 2003, and more obliquely, Read, 1993.

10   For example, Community Music has an accreditation agreement with the University of Westminster.

11   see Gelsthorpe and West-Burnham, 2003; Crowther *et al*, 2003; Rennie, 1999.

12   See Wenger (1998, pp225-277). Harvey (2000) introduces the concept of the 'insurgent architect' to suggest a praxis of agency and critical awareness; the notion of the activist teacher or organisational hacker is my attempt to explore this idea in terms more familiar to teachers.

13   introduced by Bourdieu, and elaborated by, amongst others, Putnam (1993, 2000); Baron, Field and Schuller (2001).

Bibliography

Adams, D. and Goldbard, A. (2001) *Creative Community: the art of cultural development,* New York: Rockefeller Foundation

Adams, D. and Goldbard, A. (eds) (2002) *Community, Culture and Globalisation,* New York: Rockefeller Foundation

Adey, P., Fairbrother, R., Wiliam, D. (1999) *Learning styles and strategies: a review of research,* London: King's College: Centre for the Advancement of Thinking

Alsop, A. (1999) 'The RAE and the production of knowledge', *History of the Human Sciences* 12: pp116-20

Amabile, T. (1997) *Creativity in Context: update to the Social Psychology of Creativity,* Oxford: Westview Press

Animarts (2003) *The art of the animateur,* London: Animarts

Apple, M.W. and Beane, J. (1999) *Democratic schools: lessons from the chalk face,* Buckingham: Open University Press

Apple, M.W. (2000) *Official Knowledge: democratic education in a conservative age,* London: Routledge

Aprill, A. (2002) *Finding the thread of an interrupted conversation: the arts, education and community,* online article at www.communityarts.net , accessed 15.05.03

Aprill, A., Burnaford, G. and Weiss, C. (2001) *Renaissance in the Classroom: arts integration and meaningful learning,* London: Lawrence Erlbaum Associates

Attfield, A. (1999) 'Bread and circuses? The making of Hoxton's cultural quarter and its impact on urban regeneration in Hackney', in *Rising East: the Journal of East London Studies,* Volume 1 No 3 pp133-155

Audit Commission (1998) *A fruitful partnership: effective partnership working,* London: Audit Commission

Baillie, C. (ed) (2003) *The Travelling Case: how to foster creative thinking in higher education,* Liverpool: UK Centre for Materials Education

Balloch, S. and Taylor, M. (2001) *Partnership Working: policy and practice,* Bristol: The Policy Press

Ball, S.J. (1994) *Education Reform: a critical and post-structural approach,* Buckingham: Open University Press

Ball, S.J. (1997) 'Policy critical and social research: a personal review of recent education policy and policy research', *British Education Research Journal,* 23, 3, pp257-74

Ball, S.J. (2001) 'Labour, learning and the economy' in Fielding, M (ed) (2001) *Taking education really seriously: four years hard Labour,* London: RoutledgeFalmer

Ball, S.J., Maguire, M. and Macrae, S. (2000) *Choices, transitions and pathways: new youth, new economies in the global city,* London: Falmer Press

Baron, S., Field, J. and Schuller, T. (eds) (2001) *Social Capital: critical perspectives*, Oxford: Oxford University Press

Bartlett, S. and Burton, D. (2003) 'The Management of Teachers as Professionals', in *Education Studies: essential issues*, London: Sage, pp124-138

◉ Becker, C. (1997) 'The Artist as Public Intellectual', in Giroux, H. and Shannon, P. (eds) *Education and Cultural Studies: toward a performative practice*, New York: Routledge

Beetlestone, F. (1998) *Creative Children, Imaginative Teaching*, Buckingham: Open University Press

Benjamin, A. (1999) *What's the problem?* Keynote speech at Enabling Dance – DiGM Conference, Manchester. www.adambenjamin.co.uk/documents – accessed 24.06.04

Benjamin, A. (2002) *Making an Entrance: theory and practice for disabled and non-disabled dancers*, London: Routledge

Bennett, T. (2000) *Cultural policy beyond aesthetics*, Chicago: Working Paper, University of Chicago Cultural Policy Center

Bentley, T. (1998) *Learning beyond the classroom: education for a changing world*, London: RoutledgeFalmer

Bianchini, F. and Parkinson, M. (1993) *Cultural industries and urban regeneration: the West European experience*, Manchester: Manchester University Press

Bianchini, F., Greene, L., Landry, C., Matarasso, F. (1996) *The Art of Regeneration: urban renewal through cultural activity*, Stroud: Comedia

Blake, A. and Jeffery, G. (2001a) 'Music, representation, and cultural politics in Newham', *Rising East: the Journal of East London Studies*, Vol 4 No 3, pp100-123

Blake, A. and Jeffery, G. (2001b) 'The implications of The Value of Music in London for local and regional music policy', *Cultural Trends*, issue 38, pp35-42

Bloomer, M. and Hodkinson, P. (1997) *Moving into further education: the voice of the learner*, London: Further Education Development Agency

Bloomer, M. (2001) 'Young lives, learning and transformations: some theoretical considerations', *Oxford Review of Education*, 27, 3, pp429-49

Boden, M. (ed) (1994) *Dimensions of Creativity*, Cambridge, MA: MIT Press

Bolingbroke, S. (2001) 'Employability: an ex-student's perspective', *Rising East: the journal of East London Studies*, Vol 4 No 2 pp86-99

Borden, I., Kerr, J. Rendell, J. and Pivaro, A. (eds) (2001) *The Unknown City: contesting architecture and social space*, London: MIT Press

Born, G. (1995) *Rationalising Culture: IRCAM, Boulez and the institutionalisation of the musical avant-garde*, Berkeley: University of California Press

Bosch, E. (1998) *The Pleasure of Beholding*, Barcelona: Actar

Bosch, E. (2002) *Talk and Listen*, from www.gent.be/gent/onderwijs/pbd/ basis/filosoferen%20basis/englishversion.doc (accessed 11.06.04)

Bottery, M. (1996) 'The challenge to professionals from the new public management: implications for the teaching profession', *Oxford Review of Education*, Vol 22 No 2, pp179-97

Bourdieu, P. (1976a) 'Systems of education and systems of thought', in Dale, R, Esland, G and MacDonald, M (eds) *Schooling and Capitalism: a sociological reader*, London: Routledge and Kegan Paul

Bourdieu, P. (1976b) 'The school as a conservative force: scholastic and cultural inequalities', in Dale, R, Esland, G and MacDonald, M (eds) *Schooling and Capitalism: a sociological reader*, London: Routledge and Kegan Paul

Bourdieu, P. (1984) *Distinction: a social critique of the judgement of taste*, London: Routledge

Bourdieu, P. (1993) *The field of cultural production: essays on art and literature*, Cambridge: Polity Press

Breslin, T. (2002) 'Chasing the wrong dream? The quest for teacher professionalism in the age of the citizenship school', in Johnson, M. and Hallgarten, J.: *From victims of change to agents of change: the future of the teaching profession*, London: Institute of Public Policy Research

Brice Heath, S. (1983) *Ways with Words: Language, life and work in communities and classrooms*, Cambridge: Cambridge University Press

Brice Heath, S. (1998) 'Living the arts through language and learning: a report on community-based youth organisations', Washington DC: *Americans for the Arts monographs*, Vol 2 No 7

Brice Heath, S. (2004) Unpublished introduction to seminar paper on 'Creativity, the Arts and Achievement'

Brice Heath, S. and McLaughlin, M. (eds) (1993) *Identity and inner-city youth: beyond ethnicity and gender*, New York: Teachers College Press

Brice Heath, S. and McLaughlin, M. (1994) 'Learning for anything every day', *Journal of curriculum Studies* 26, p.471-89

Brice Heath, S. and Roach, A. (1998) The arts in the non-school hours: strategic opportunities for meeting the education, civic learning, and job-training goals of America's youth, unpublished briefing materials for the President's committee on the Arts and the Humanities

Brice Heath, S. and Robinson, K. (2004) 'Making a way: youth arts and learning in international perspective' pp107-127 in Rabkin, N. and Redmond, R. *Putting the Arts in the Picture: Reframing education in the 21st century*, Chicago: Columbia College

Brice Heath, S. and Smyth, L. (1999) *ArtShow: Youth and Community Development*, Washington, DC: Partners for Livable Communities

Brice Heath, S. and Wolf, S. (2004a) *Visual learning in the community school*, London: Creative Partnerships

Brice Heath, S. and Wolf, S. (2004b) *Hoping for accidents: media and technique, part 2 of, Visual learning in the community school*, London: Creative Partnerships

Brighouse, T. (2002) *Comprehensive Schools now, then and in the future – is it time to draw a line in the sand and create a new ideal?* The Caroline Benn, Brian Simon Memorial Lecture, London: Institute of Education

British Academy, (2004) *'That full compliment of Riches': the contribution of the arts, humanities and social sciences to the nation's wealth*, London: British Academy

British Council (2003) *Arts for culture and development: In Profile 2003* http://www2.british council.org/arts-performing-arts-acd-directory.htm accessed 03.09.04

Brooke-Smith, R. (2003) *Leading learners, leading schools*, London: RoutledgeFalmer

Burke, C. and Grosvenor, I. (2003) *The School I'd Like: children and young people's reflections on education for the 21st century*, London: RoutledgeFalmer

Butler. T. (ed) (2000) *Eastern Promise: Education and social renewal in London's Docklands*, London: Lawrence and Wishart

Butler, T. and Rustin, M. (1996) *Rising in the East: the regeneration of east London*, London: Lawrence and Wishart

Buzan, T. (2002) *How to Mind Map: the ultimate thinking tool that will change your life*, London: HarperCollins

Buzan, T. and Buzan, B. (2003) *The Mind Map Book: Radiant Thinking – Major Evolution in Human Thought*, London: BBC Books

Caine, N.R., and Caine, G (1997) *Education on the edge of possibility*, Alexandria, Virginia: Association for Supervision and Curriculum Development

Carley, M., Chapman, M., Hastings, A., Kirk, K., and Young, R. (2000) *Urban regeneration through partnership: a study in nine urban regions in England, Scotland and Wales*, Bristol: The Policy Press

Carr, W. and Hartnett, A. (1996) *Education and the struggle for democracy*, Buckingham: Open University Press

Carter, R. (2004) *Language and Creativity: the art of common talk*, London: Routledge

Casey, C. (1995) *Work, Self and Society: After industrialism*, London: Routledge

Castells, M. (1989) *The informational city*, Oxford, Blackwell

Castells, M. (2004) 'Space of flows, space of places: materials for a theory of urbanism in the information age', in Graham, S. (ed) *The Cybercities Reader*, London: Routledge

Castells, M. and Himanen, P. (2002) *The Information Society and the Welfare State: The Finnish Model*, Cambridge: Cambridge University Press

Catterall, J.S., Hetland, L., and Winner, E. (eds) (2002) *Critical Links: Learning in the Arts and Student Academic and Social development*, Washington DC: Arts Education Partnership

CBI (1989) *Towards a skills revolution*, London: Confederation of British Industry

CBI (1993) *Routes for success: Careerships, a strategy for all 16-19 learning*, London: Confederation of British Industry

Centre for Creative Communities (2004) *Creative community-building through cross-sector collaboration*, London: Centre for Creative Communities

Clark, B. (2004) *Sustaining change in universities: continuities in case studies and concepts*, Maidenhead: Open University Press

Claxton, G. (2000) *Wise Up! The challenge of lifelong learning*, London: Bloomsbury

Claxton, G. and Lucas, B. (2002) *Be Creative: essential steps to revitalise your work and life*, London: BBC Books

de Certeau, M., Giard, L., Mayol, P., (2002) *The Practice of Everyday Life*, Los Angeles: University of California Press

de Certeau, M. (1994) *Culture in the Plural*, Minneapolis: University of Minnesota Press

Coffield, F., Moseley, D., Hall, E., Ecclestone, K. (2004) *Should we be using learning styles? What research has to say to practice*, London: Learning and Skills Development Agency

Cohen, P. (1996) *Rethinking the Youth Question: education, labour and cultural studies*, London: Palgrave Macmillan

Cohen, P. (1997b) 'Out of the melting pot and into the fire next time: Imagining the East End as city, body, text', in Westwood, S. and Williams, J. *Imagining Cities: Scripts, Signs, Memory*, London: Routledge

Cohen, P. (1998) 'The Road to Beckton Pier?' in *Rising East: the Journal of East London Studies*, Vol. 1 No 3 pp24-51

Coren, M. (1984) *Theatre Royal: 100 Years of Stratford East*, London: Quartet Books

Corker, M. and Shakespeare, T. (2002) *Disability/Postmodernity: Embodying Disability Theory*, London: Continuum

Cornwall, A. and Pratt, G. (eds) (2003) *Pathways to Participation: reflections on participatory rural appraisal*, London: Intermediate Technology Development Group

Coult, T. and Kershaw, B. (1990) *Engineers of the Imagination: the Welfare State Handbook*, London: Methuen

Craft, A. (1996) 'Nourishing Educator Creativity: a holistic approach to CPD', *British Journal of In-Service Education*, Vol 22 No 3, pp209-22

Craft, A. (2000) *Continuing Professional Development: a practical guide for teachers and schools (2nd edition)*, London: Routledge

Craft, A. (2000) *Creativity Across the Curriculum: framing and developing practice*, London: Routledge

Craft, A. (2001) 'Little c creativity' in Craft, A., Jeffrey, B. and Leibling, M. *Creativity in Education*, London: Continuum

Craft, A. (2003) 'The limits to creativity in education: dilemmas for the educator', *British Journal of Educational Studies*, Vol 51 No 2, pp113-27

Craft, A. (in press) *Creativity in Schools: Tensions and Dilemmas*, London: RoutledgeFalmer

Craft, A., Jeffrey, B. and Liebling, M. (eds) (2001) *Creativity in Education*, London: Continuum

Creigh-Tyte, A. and Thomas, B. (2001) 'Employment' in Selwood, S. (ed) *The UK Cultural Sector, Profile and Policy Issues*, London: Policy Studies Institute

Crowther, D., Cummings, C., Dyson, A. and Millward, A. (2003) *Schools and area regeneration*, Bristol: The Policy Press

Csikzsentmihalyi, M. (1997) *Living Well: the psychology of everyday life*, London: Phoenix

Csikzsentmihalyi, M. (1998) 'Society, culture and person: a systems view of creativity' in Sternberg, R. (ed) *The Nature of Creativity*, Cambridge: Cambridge University Press

Csikszentmihalyi, M. (2003) *Good Business: Leadership, flow and the making of meaning*, London: Hodder and Stoughton

Czerniawska, B. (1997) *Narrating the Organisation*, Chicago: University of Chicago Press

Dadds, M. (1995) *Passionate Inquiry and school development: a story about teacher action research*, London: Falmer Press

Dadds, M. and Hart, S. (2001) *Doing Practitioner Research Differently*, London: Routledge Falmer

Daly, A. (2004) *Richard Florida's High Class Glasses*, from http://www.anndaly.com/articles/florida.html, accessed 14.09.04

Dartington College of Arts (2004) *Connections and Collaborations: developing higher education's continuing professional development provision for arts and design practitioners*, Dartington: Dartington College of Arts and Falmouth College of Arts

Dash, P. (1999) 'Thoughts on a relevant art curriculum for the 21st Century', *International Journal of Art and Design Education*, Vol 18, No. 1, p. 123

Davenport, T.H. and Prusack, L. (1997) *Working knowledge; how organisations manage what they know*, Cambridge: Harvard Business School Press

Davies, R. and Lindley, R. (2003) *Artists in figures: a statistical portrait of cultural occupations*, London: Arts Council England

DCMS (1998) *Creative Industries Mapping Document*, London: HMSO

DCMS (2001) *Culture and Creativity: the next ten years*, London: HMSO

DCMS (2004a) *Culture at the heart of regeneration*, London: HMSO

DCMS (2004b) *Leading the Good Life. Guidance on Integrating Cultural and Community Strategies*, London: HMSO

Deer, C. (2003) 'Bourdieu on Higher Education: the meaning of the growing integration of educational systems and self-reflective practice', *British Journal of Sociology of Education*, Vol 24, No 2, pp195-207

DfEE (1997) *Qualifying for Success*, London, HMSO

DfEE (1998) *The Learning Age: a renaissance for a new Britain*, London: HMSO

DfES (2003) *Success for All*, London: HMSO

DfES (2004a) *Five year strategy for children and learners: putting people at the heart of public services,* London: HMSO

DfES (2004b) *Music Manifesto,* London: HMSO. See also www.musicmanifesto.co.uk

DfES (2004c) *A National Conversation about Personalised Learning,* London: HMSO

Deprez, F.L. and Tissen, R (2002) *Zero Space: Moving beyond organisational limits,* San Francisco: Berrett-Koehler Publishers, InDETR (2003) *Indices of Local Deprivation,* London: HMSOc.

Dewey, J. (1973) 'Education as Growth' in Silberman, C. *The Open Classroom reader,* New York, Random House, pp121-131

Dewulf, S. and Baillie, C. (1999) *Creativity in Art, Science and Engineering: how to foster creativity,* London: DfES

DiMaggio, P. and Powell, W. (1983) 'The Iron Cage revisited: Institutional isomorphism and collective rationality in organizational fields' *American Sociological Review* 38: pp147-60

Dougherty, K. (1994) *The contradictory college: the conflicting origins, impacts and futures of the community college,* Albany: State University of New York Press

Doyle, M. (2004) Partnership practices and complexities of collaboration, unpublished paper given at BERA Conference, September 2004

Dust, K. (1999) *Motive, Means and Opportunity: NESTA research review,* NESTA (from www.nesta.org.uk, accessed 11.10.02)

Eade, J. (ed) (1997) *Living the Global City: globalisation as local process,* London: Routledge

Eames, P. (2003) *Creative Solutions and Social Inclusion: culture and the community,* Wellington, NZ: Steele Roberts

Ecclestone, K. (2002) *Learning autonomy in post-16 education: the politics and practice of formative assessment,* London: RoutledgeFalmer

Eisner, E. (1972) *Educating Artistic Vision,* New York: Macmillan

Eisner, E. (1990) 'Discipline-based arts education: conceptions and misconceptions', *Educational Theory* 40(4), 423-430

Eisner, E. (2004) *The Arts and the Creation of Mind,* New Haven: Yale University Press

Eraut, M. (2000) 'Informal learning, implicit learning and tacit knowledge in professional work', in Coffield, F. (ed) (2000) *The Necessity of Informal Learning,* Bristol: the Policy Press

Evans, G. and Foord, J. (2004) 'Shaping the Cultural Landscape: Local regeneration effects', in Miles, M. and Hall, T. (eds) *Urban Futures: critical commentaries on shaping the city,* London: Routledge

Everitt, A. (1997) *Joining In: an investigation into participatory music,* London: Gulbenkian Foundation

European Commission (1998) *Social indicators: problematic issues,* Brussels: European Commission

Feldman, D.H., Csikszentmihalyi, M., Gardner, H. (1994) *Changing the world: a framework for the study of creativity,* London: Praeger Publishers

Ferguson, R., Glover, M. Minh-ha, T., and West, C. (eds) (1990) *Out there: marginalization and contemporary cultures,* London, MIT Press

FEFC (2000) *Newham Sixth Form College: a report by the inspectorate,* Coventry: Further Education Funding Council

Fielding, M. (1998) 'Empowerment: emancipation or enervation?' *Journal of Education Policy,* Vol 11 No 2, pp399-417

Fielding, M. (1999a) 'Myth: schools are communities', in O'Hagan, B. (ed) (1999) *Modern Educational Myths: the future of democratic comprehensive education,* London: Kogan Page

Fielding, M. (1999b) 'Radical collegiality: affirming teaching as an inclusive professional practice,' *Australian Educational Researcher* Vol 26 No2, pp1-34

Fielding, M. (ed) (2001) *Taking education really seriously: four years hard Labour*, London: Routledge-Falmer

Figueiredo-Cowen, M. and Gastaldo, D. (1995) *Paulo Freire at the Institute of Education*, London: Institute of Education, London: Institute of Education

Fine, B. (2000) *Social Capital versus Social Theory: Political Economy and Social Science at the Turn of the Millennium*, London: Routledge

Finegold, D., Keep, E., Miliband, D., Raffe, D., Spours, K., and Young, M. (1990) *A British Baccalaureate: overcoming divisions between education and training*, London: Institute for Public Policy Research

Finnegan, R. (1989) *The Hidden Musicians: music-making in an English town*, Cambridge: Cambridge University Press

Fisher, K, and Fisher, M.D. (1998) *The Distributed Mind: achieving high performance through the collective intelligence of knowledge work teams*, New York: American Management Association

Fiske, E. (1999) *Champions of Change: The Impact of the Arts on Learning*, Washington DC: Arts Education Partnership and the President's Committee on the Arts and the Humanities

Florida, R. (2002) *The Rise of the Creative Class, and how it's transforming work, leisure, community and everyday life*, New York: Basic Books

Ford Foundation (2003) *Downside Up: Listening Tour, Final Report*, New York: Ford Foundation

Foucault, M. (1973) *The Birth of the Clinic*, London: Routledge

Foucault, M. (1979) *Discipline and Punish: the birth of the prison*, Harmondsworth: Penguin Books

Foucault, M. (1982) *The Archaeology of Knowledge*, London: Pantheon Books

Fox, J. (2002) *Eyes on Stalks*, London: Methuen

Freire, P. (1970) *Pedagogy of the Oppressed*, New York: Herder and Herder

Freire, P. (1998a) *Pedagogy of Freedom: ethics, democracy and civic courage*, Oxford: Rowman and Littlefield

Freire, P. (1998b) *Pedagogy of Hope*, London: Continuum

Fryer, M. (1996) *Creative teaching and learning*, London: Paul Chapman

Fullan, M. (2001) *Leading in a culture of change*, San Francisco: Jossey-Bass/Wiley

Fyfe, H. (2002) *She Danced... and We Danced: artists, creativity and education*, Belfast: The Stranmillis Press

Gablik, S. (1991) *The re-enchantment of art*, London: Thames and Hudson

Gale, T. and Densmore, K. (2000) *Just Schooling: Explorations in the Cultural Politics of Teaching*, Buckingham: Open University Press

Gale, T., and Densmore, K. (2003) *Engaging Teachers: towards a radical democratic agenda for schooling*, Buckingham: Open University Press

Gardiner, R. and Peggie, A. (2003) *All Together Now? Opportunities in youth music making: a practitioner guide to project and funding opportunities within youth, cultural. educational and social regeneration agencies*, London: Youth Music

Gardner, H. (1983) *Frames of Mind*, London: Fontana

Gardner, H. (1991) *The Unschooled Mind: How children think and how schools should teach*, New York: Basic Books

Gardner, H. (1993) *Multiple Intelligences: the theory in practice*, New York: Basic Books

Gardner, H. (2000) *The Disciplined Mind: beyond facts and standardized tests, the K-12 education that every child deserves*, London: Penguin

Gardner, H., Csikszentmihalyi, M. and Damon, W. (2001) *Good Work: where excellence and ethics meet*, New York: Basic Books

Gatto, J. (ed) (2002) *The Exhausted School*, Berkeley: Berkeley Hills Books

Geer, R.O. (1993) 'Of the People, by the People, for the People: the field of community performance', *High Performance*, winter 1993, pp24-28

Gelsthorpe, T. and West-Burnham, J. (2003) *Educational Leadership and the Community: strategies for school improvement through community engagement*, London: Pearson Education

Gibbons, M., Limoges, C., Nowotny, H., Schwarzman, S. , Scott, P. and Trow, M. (1994) *The New Production of Knowledge: the dynamics of science and research in contemporary societies*, London: Sage

Gillborn, D. and Ladson-Billings, G. (eds) (2004): *Reader in Multicultural Education: Critical Perspectives on Race, Racism and Education*, London: RoutledgeFalmer

Giroux, H. (1981) *Ideology, culture and the process of schooling*, London: Falmer

Giroux, H. and Shannon, P. (eds) (1997) *Education and Cultural Studies: toward a performative practice*, New York: Routledge

Glatter, R. (ed) (1989) *Educational institutions and their environments: managing the boundaries*, Milton Keynes: Open University Press

Glendinning, C., Powell, M, and Rummery, K. (2002) *Partnerships, New Labour and the Governance of Welfare*, Bristol: The Policy Press

Gordon, I. (1996) 'Family structure, educational achievement and the inner city', *Urban Studies*, Vol 33 No 8, pp1395-1406

Gould, H. (2004) *Developing the role of the arts in UK social policy: a discussion paper*, London: Creative Exchange

Government Office for London (GOL) (2001) *London Objective 2 Programme 2001-2006: single programming document*, London, GOL

Graham, S. and Marvin, S. (2001) *Splintering Urbanism: networked infrastructures, technological mobilities and the urban condition*, London: Routledge

Green, L. (2001) *How Popular Musicians Learn: a way ahead for music education*, Aldershot: Ashgate

Hall, S. and du Gay, P. (1996) *Questions of cultural identity*, London: Sage

Hall, P. (1999) *Cities in Civilization: culture, innovation and urban order*, London: Phoenix Giant

Hamnett, C. (2003) *Unequal City: London in the global arena*, London: Routledge

Handy, C. (1999) *The New Alchemists*, London: Hutchinson

Harber, C. (1992) *Democratic Learning and Learning Democracy*, Ticknall: Education Now

Harber, C. and Meighan, R. (1989) *The Democratic School*, Ticknall: Education Now

Hargreaves, A. (1994) *Changing Teachers, Changing Times; teachers' work and culture in the postmodern age*, London: Cassell

Hargreaves, A. (2003) *Teaching in the knowledge society*, Maidenhead: Open University Press

Hargreaves, D.H. (1998) *Creative professionalism: the role of teachers in the knowledge society*, London: Demos

Hargreaves, D.H. (2003) *Working laterally: how innovation networks make an education epidemic*, London: Demos/DfES

Harland, J., Kinder, K. Lord, P. Stott, A., Schagen, I., Haynes, J, with Cusworth, L., White, R. and Paola, R. (2000): *Arts education in secondary schools: effects and effectiveness*, Slough: NFER

Harvey, D. (1988) *Social Justice and the City*, Oxford: Blackwell

Harvey, D. (1989) *The Urban Experience*, Baltimore, Johns Hopkins Press

Harvey, D. (2000) *Spaces of Hope*, Edinburgh: Edinburgh University Press

Hawkes, J. (2001) *The Fourth Pillar of Sustainability: culture's essential role in public planning*, Victoria: Cultural Development Network

HEFCE (2003) *Circular 15: Good practice: Supporting higher education in further education colleges: a guide for tutors and lecturers*, London: HEFCE

HEFCE (2003) *Circular 16: Good practice: Supporting higher education in further education colleges: policy, practice and prospects*, London: HEFCE

Hobsbawn, E. and Ranger, T. (1983) *The invention of tradition*, Cambridge: Cambridge University Press

Hodgson, A. and Spours, K. (1999) *New Labour's education agenda: issues and policies for education and training from 14+*, London: Kogan Page

Hodkinson, P., Sparkes, A. and Hodkinson, H. (1996) *Triumphs and tears: young people, markets and the transition from school to work*, London: David Fulton

Holt, J. (1977) *Instead of education: ways to help people do things better*, London: Pelican

hooks, b. (1989) *Talking Back: Thinking Feminist – Thinking Black*, Boston, MA: South End Press

Horne M. and Jones D.S. (2002) *Leadership: the challenge for all? Executive Summary* London: Institute of Management

Huberman, M. (1989) 'The model of the independent artisan in teachers' professional development', in Little, J.W. and McLaughlin, M.W. (eds) *Teachers Work: Individuals, Colleagues and Contexts*, New York: Teachers College Press

Hughes, M. (2003) *Successful engagement: guidance for colleges and providers in effective employer engagement in post-16 learning*, London: LSDA

Huxham, C. (2000) 'The Challenge of Collaborative Governance', *Public Management*, Vol. 2 No 3, pp337-357

Huxham, C. and Vangen, S. (2003) *Doing things collaboratively: realising the advantage or succumbing to inertia?* Glasgow: University of Strathclyde Graduate School of Business Working Papers Series: 11

ICM (2002) *Barriers to the realisation of creative ideas: management summary*, London: NESTA

Illich, I. (1973) *Deschooling Society*, Harmondsworth: Penguin

Ings, R. (2002) *The arts included*, London: Arts Council of England

Ings, R. (2004) *The inventive answer? Thoughts on creativity and young people*, London: NESTA

Itzin, C. (1980) *Stages in the Revolution*, London: Eyre, Methuen

Jackson, T. (1993) *Learning through Theatre: new perspectives on theatre and education*, London: Routledge

Jeffery, B. (2004) *The artist, the teacher and creative teaching and learning*, Milton Keynes: Open University, from http://opencreativity.open.ac.uk/current-projects.cfm?sm=projects& pg=current-projects, accessed 19.09.04

Jeffery, B. and Woods, p(2003) *The Creative School: a framework for success, quality and effectiveness*, London: RoutledgeFalmer.

Jensen, K. and Walker, S. (eds) (1989) *Towards Democratic Schooling: European Experiences*, Buckingham: Open University Press.

Johnson, G. (2004) *New Audiences for the Arts*, London: Arts Council England

Johnstone, D. (2003) *Partnerships: benefits, limitations, and doing it better*, London, LSDA

Jowell, T. (2004) *Government and the Value of Culture*, London: HMSO

Kearney, C. (2003) *The Monkey's Mask: Identity, Memory, Narrative and Voice*, Stoke on Trent: Trentham Books

Kennedy, H. (1997) *Learning Works: widening participation in further education*, Coventry: Further Education Funding Council

Kershaw, B. (1992) *The Politics of Performance: radical theatre as cultural intervention*, London: Routledge

Kershaw, B. (1999) *The Radical in Performance: between Brecht and Baudrillard*, London: Routledge

Kester, G. (1999) *Socially engaged practice-dialogical aesthetics: a critical framework for Littoral Art*, available from http://www.variant.randomstate.org/9texts/KesterSupplement.html

Kester, G. (2004) *Conversation Pieces: community and communication in modern art*, Los Angeles: University of California Press

Keys, S. (2003) 'Accessible counselling', *Association of University and College Counsellors Newsletter*, Winter 2003

Kinder, K. and Harland, J (2004) 'The arts and social inclusion: what's the evidence?' *Support for Learning*, Vol 19 No 2, pp52-56

Kretzmann, J. and McKnight, J. (1993) *Building Communities from the Inside Out: a path toward finding and mobilizing a community's assets*, Chicago: Northwestern University Institute for Policy Research

Kuppers, P. (2003) *Disability and performance: bodies on the edge*, London: Routledge

Kushner, S. (1994) 'Against better judgement: how a centrally prescribed music curriculum works against teacher development', *International Journal of Music Education* Vol 23, pp34-45

Lago, G. and Shipton, G. (1995) *Personal Tutoring in Action*, Sheffield: Sheffield University Counselling Service

Landry, C. (2000) *The Creative City: a toolkit for urban innovators*, London: Earthscan

Landry, C. and Matarasso, F. (1998) *The Learning City-Region: Approaching problems of the concept, its measurement and evaluation*, Paris: OECD

Landry, C. and Pachter, M. (2001) *Culture at the Crossroads: Culture and cultural institutions at the beginning of the 21st Century*, Stroud: Comedia

Lave, J. (1991) *Situated Learning: legitimate peripheral participation*, Cambridge: Cambridge University Press

LDA (2003) *Understanding London's sub-regional economies*, London: LDA

LDA (2004a) *Creative London: report of the Mayor's Commission on the Creative Industries*, London: LDA

LDA (2004b) *Mapping BME-led Creative Industries in London: a final report*, London: LDA

Leadbeater, C. (2000) *Living on Thin Air: the new economy*, London: Penguin Books

Leibel, M. (2004) *A Will of Their Own: cross cultural perspectives on working children*, London: Zed Books

Lerman, L. (2002) *Dancing in Community: its roots in art: Community Arts Network*, www.communityarts.net, accessed 13.09.03

Lerman, L. and Borstel, J. (2003) *Critical Response Process: a method for getting useful feedback on anything you make from dance to dessert,* Washington, DC: Liz Lerman Dance Exchange

Liebenthal, A., Feinstein, O.N., Ingram. G.K. (2004) *Evaluation and development: the partnership dimension,* London: Transaction Publishers

Lingard, B., Hayes, D., Mills, M. and Christie, P. (2003) *Leading Learning: making hope practical in schools,* Maidenhead: Open University Press

Lippard, L. R. (1997) *The Lure of the Local: senses of place in a multicentred society,* New York: The New Press

LSDA (2003) *Learning and skills for neighbourhood renewal: a policy review,* London: LSDA

LSDA (2004) *Learning brokerage in the workplace: some preliminary reflections,* London: LSDA

Lucas, B. and Greany, T. (2000) *Schools in the Learning Age,* London: Southgate

MacBeath, J. (2003) *Leadership: learning to live with contradiction,* Nottingham: National College for School Leadership

Macgregor, L., Tate, M., and Robinson, K. (1979) *Learning through Drama (Schools Council Drama Teaching Project: 10-16),* London: Heinemann

Macrae, S., Maguire, M. and Ball, S. (1997) 'Whose learning society? A tentative deconstruction' *Education Policy* Vol 12, pp499-509

Mahony, P. and Hextall, I. (2000) *Reconstructing Teaching: standards, performance and accountability,* London: RoutledgeFalmer

Marks, V. (1998) Programme note for *Sites Pacific,* performed at the opening of the Getty Center in Los Angeles.

Marquand, D. (1992) 'The Enterprise Culture: Old Wine in New Bottles?' in Heelas, P. and Morris, P. (eds) *The Values of the Enterprise Culture: the moral debate,* London: Routledge

Matarasso, F. (1997) *Use or Ornament? The Social Impact of Participation in the Arts,* Stroud: Comedia

Maury, L. and Freinet, C. (1993) *Freinet et la Pedagogie,* Paris: Presses Universitaires de France

Mayo, M. (1997) 'Partnerships for regeneration and community development' in *Critical Social Policy,* Vol 17 No 3, pp3-26

Mayor of London (2003) *London: Cultural Capital,* London: Greater London Authority

Mayor of London (2004) *London: Cultural Capital. Realising the Potential of a World-Class City,* London: Greater London Authority

McNorton, J. (2002) 'Choreography of Drawing: The Consciousness of the Body in the Space of a Drawing', *International Journal of Art and Design Education,* Vol 21 No 3. pp254-257

Meighan, R. and Toogood, P. (1992) *Anatomy of Choice in Education,* Ticknall: Education Now

Middleton, R. (1990) *Studying Popular Music,* Milton Keynes: Open University Press

Miliband, D. (2004) *Choice and Voice in Personalised Learning,* http://www.DfES.gov.uk/speeches/search_detail.cfm?ID=118, accessed 23.07.04

Mitchell, W. (1999) *City of Bits; Space, Place and the Infobahn,* London: MIT Press

Moon, B. (1983) *Comprehensive Schools: challenge and change,* London: NFER Nelson

Muschamp, P. (2004) 'Arts education: an OfSTED perspective' in Cowling, J. (ed) (2004) *For Art's Sake? Society and the Arts in the 21st Century,* London: Institute of Public Policy Research

National Advisory Committee on Creativity, Culture and Education (1999) *All Our Futures: creativity, culture and education,* London: HMSO

National Audit Office (2003) *Progress on 15 Major Capital Projects funded by Arts Council England,* London: HMSO

Nelson, C.A. (2001) *The Arts and Education Reform: lessons from a four-year evaluation of the A+ Schools, 1995-1999* Winston-Salem, NC: Kenan Institute

Neperud, R. (ed) (1996) 'Context, content and community in art education, beyond post-modernism', in Efland, A. *Change in the conceptions of art teaching*, New York: Teachers College Press

Newham Household Panel Survey 2002, London: London Borough of Newham

Newham in Profile 2003/4, London: London Borough of Newham

NewVIc (1992) *Prospectus for full time students*, London: Newham Sixth Form College

Nind, M, Rix, J., Sheehy, K. and Simmons, K. (2003) *Inclusive education: diverse perspectives*, London: David Fulton

Norris, C. (ed) (1989) *Music and the Politics of Culture*, London: Lawrence and Wishart

Office of Community Arts Partnerships (2002) *Urban Missions: Program and Process Guide*, Chicago, OCAP

O'Connor, J. (1999) *The Definition of Cultural Industries*, available at www.mmu.ac.uk/h-ss/mipc/iciss/reports/defin.pdf, accessed 13.01.04

O'Hagan, B. (1991) *The Charnwood Papers: fallacies in community education*, Ticknall: Education Now

O'Neill, O. (2002) *A Question of Trust: the BBC Reith Lectures 2002*, Cambridge: Cambridge University Press

OECD (2004) *Innovation in the Knowledge Economy: implications for education and learning*, Paris: OECD

Ofsted (1998) *The Arts Inspected*, London: HMSO

Ofsted (1999) *Artists in Schools*, London: HMSO

Ofsted (2003a) *Improving City Schools: how the arts can help*, HMI 1709, London: HMSO

Ofsted (2003b) *Expecting the Unexpected: developing creativity in primary and secondary schools*, HMI 1612, London: HMSO

Ofsted (2003c) *Inspection report: Newham Local Education Authority*, London: HMSO

Ofsted/FEFC (1999) *Post-16 collaboration: school sixth forms and the further education sector: a joint report by the Ofsted and FEFC inspectorate*, Coventry: FEFC

Orr, D. (2004) *Earth in Mind: on Education, Environment and the Human Prospect*, New York: Island Press

Parkes, J. and Califano, A. (2004) *Home: an educational resource pack*, London: NewVIc New Media

Parkes, J. and Connor, C. (2004) *People Moving: towards an integrated learning culture for dance*, London: East London Dance

Paynter, J. (1992) *Sound and Structure*, Cambridge: Cambridge University Press

Pearson, J. (2002) *University-community design partnerships: innovations in practice*, Washington DC: National Endowment for the Arts

Perkins, D. (1992) *Smart schools: From Training Memories to Educating Minds*, New York: Free Press

Perkins, D. (1995) *Outsmarting IQ: The Emerging Science of Learnable Intelligence*, New York: The Free Press

Perkins, D. (1999) 'The many faces of constructivism', *Educational Leadership* Vol 57 No 3, pp6-11

Portes, A. (1998) 'Social Capital: its origins and application in modern sociology', *Annual Review of Sociology* Vol 24, pp1-24

Power, M. (1994) *The Audit Explosion*, London: Demos

Public Services Productivity Panel (2002) *Working Together: Effective Partnership Working on the Ground*, London: HMSO

Putnam, R. (1993) *Making Democracy Work*, Princeton, NJ: Princeton University Press

Putnam, R. (2001) *Bowling Alone: the collapse and revival of American community*, London: Simon and Schuster

Putnam, R., Feldstein, L. and Cohen, L. (2003) *Better Together: restoring the American community*, London: Simon and Schuster

Raggatt, P. and Williams, S. (1999) *Government, markets and vocational qualifications: an anatomy of policy*, London: Falmer Press

Read, A. (1993) *Theatre and Everyday Life: an ethics of performance*, London: Routledge

Reimer, E. (1971) *School is Dead*, London: Pelican

Rennie, J. (1999) *Branching Out: schools as community regenerators*, Coventry; Community Education Development Centre

Renshaw, P. (2003) *Connecting conversations: the changing voice of the artist*, Amsterdam: European League of Institutes of the Arts

Robinson, K. (ed) (1982) *The Arts in Schools: principles, practice and provision*, London: Calouste Gulbenkian Foundation

Robinson, K. (ed) (1990) *The Arts 5-16: a Curriculum Framework*, Essex: Oliver and Boyd

Robinson, K. (2001) *Out of our minds: learning to be creative*, Oxford: Capstone

Ross, M. (2003) 'Evaluating education programmes in arts organisations', *Music Education Research*, Vol 5 No 1, pp69-79

Sachs, J. (2003a) *The Activist Teaching Profession*, Buckingham: Open University Press

Sachs, J. (2003b) Teacher Activism: mobilising the profession, paper given at British Educational Research Association annual conference, Southwell: BERA

Sakolsky, R. and Wei-han Ho, F. (eds) (1995) *Sounding Off: Music as subversion/resistance/revolution*, New York: Autonomedia

Sands, J. (2000) *A convivial culture for health? Case studies in holistic practice*, available from www.newvic-creative.org.uk

Sasaki, M. (2004) *The role of culture in urban regeneration*, Barcelona: Forum Barcelona

Sassen, S. (1996) 'Rebuilding the global city: economy, ethnicity and space', in King, A. (ed): *Representing the City: Ethnicity, capital and culture in the 21st century metropolis*, New York: New York University Press

Sassen, S. (1999) *Globalization and its discontents*, New York: New Press

Sassen, S. (2001) *The Global City: New York, London Tokyo* (2nd ed.), Princeton, NJ: Princeton University Press

Schon, D. (1983) *The reflective practitioner: how professionals think in action*, London: Temple Smith

Sefton-Green, J. (ed) (1999) *Creativity, Young People and New Technologies: the Challenge of Digital Arts*, London: Routledge

Seidel, S., Eppel, M., Martiniello, M. (2001) *Arts Survive: A Study of Sustainability in Arts Education Partnerships*, Cambridge, MA: Project Zero at the Harvard Graduate School of Education

Seltzer, K. and Bentley, T (1999) *The Creative Age: knowledge and skills for the new economy*, London: Demos

Senge, P. (1990) *The Fifth Discipline: the art and practice of the learning organisation*, London: Random House

Senge P., Cambron-McCabe, N, Lucas, T., Smith, B., Dutton, J. and Kleiner, A (2000) *Schools that Learn: a fifth discipline fieldbook for educators, parents and everyone who cares about education*, London: Nicholas Brealey

Sennett, R. (1998) *The Corrosion of Character; the personal consequences of work in the new capitalism*, London: Norton

Sergiovanni, T. (2000) 'Changing change: towards a design and art', *Journal of Educational Change* Vol 1 No 1, p57-75

Sharma, A., Sharma, S. and Hutnyk, J. (eds) (1996) *Dis-orienting Rhythms: the politics of the New Asian Dance Music*, London: Zed Books

Shakespeare, T. (ed) (2000) *The Disability Reader*, London: Continuum

Sharp, C. and Dust, K. (1997) *Artists in schools: a handbook for teachers and artists*, Slough: National Foundation for Educational Research

Sharp, C. and Le Metais, J. (2000) *The arts, creativity and cultural education: an international perspective*, London: QCA

Shaw, P. (2001) *Creative Connections: business and the arts working together for a more inclusive society*, London; Arts and Business

Shepherd, J. (1991) *Music as Social Text*, London: Polity Press

Shils, E. (1981) *Tradition*, London: Faber

Shore, C. and Wright, S. (eds) (1997) *Anthropology of Policy: Critical perspectives on governance and power*, London: Routledge

Shore, C. and Wright, S. (2000) 'Coercive accountability: the rise of audit culture in higher education' in Strathern, M. (ed) *Audit Cultures*, London: Routledge

Short, E. (1991) *Forms of Curriculum Enquiry*, New York: SUNY Press

Silberman, E. (ed) (1973) *The Open Classroom Reader*, New York: Random House

Simpson, J. (2002) *Community arts meets higher education*, from www.artslearning partnership.org.uk, accessed 17.02.04

Smith, C. (1998) *Creative Britain*, London: Faber

Smith, N. (1996) *The New Urban Frontier: gentrification and the revanchist city*, London: Routledge

Stenhouse, L. (1967) *Culture and education*, London; Nelson

Stenhouse, L. (1983) *Authority, education and emancipation*, London: Heinemann

Stenhouse, L. (1986) 'Curriculum research, artistry and teaching', in Rudduck, J. and Hopkins, D. *Research as a basis for teaching: readings from the work of Lawrence Stenhouse*, London: Heinemann

Sternberg, R. (1988) *The nature of creativity: contemporary psychological perspectives*, Cambridge: Cambridge University Press

Sternberg, R. (1997) *Thinking Styles*, Cambridge: Cambridge University Press

Strathern, M. (ed) (2000) *Audit cultures*, London: Routledge

Swain, J. and French, S. (2003) 'Towards an Affirmation Model of Disability', Chapter 14 in Nind, M, Rix, J., Sheehy, K. and Simmons, K. (2003): *Inclusive education: diverse perspectives*, London: David Fulton Publishers

Swartz, D. (1997) *Culture and Power: the sociology of Pierre Bourdieu*, Chicago: University of Chicago Press

Tate, N. (1999) 'What is education for?' *English in Education* Vol 33 No 2 p5-18

Timms, S. (1998) 'East London and the new Labour government', *Rising East, the Journal of East London Studies*, Vol 1 No 3, p87-105

Tomlinson, M. (2004) *14-19 Curriculum and Qualifications Reform: Final Report of the Working Group on 14-19 Reform*, London: HMSO

Toogood, P. and Meighan, R. (1992) *Anatomy of Choice in Education*, Ticknall: Education Now

Torrance, E. P. (ed) (2000) *On the Edge and Keeping on the Edge*, Westwood: Ablex

Toynbee, J. (2000) *Making Popular Music: musicians, creativity and institutions*, London: Arnold

Trend, D. (1997) 'The fine art of teaching' in Giroux H.A. and Shannon, P. (eds): *Education and Cultural Studies: towards a performative practice*, London: Routledge

Troman, G. and Woods, P. (2001) *The social construction of teacher stress*, London: Routledge

Tuckman, B.W. (1965) 'Developmental sequence in small groups', *Psychological Bulletin*, Vol. 63, p284-389

Tufnel, M. and Crickmay, C. (1993) *Body Space Image: notes towards improvisation and performance*, London: Dance Books

UNESCO (2004) Preliminary Draft Convention on the protection of the diversity of cultural contents and artistic expressions, Paris: UNESCO

von Stamm, B. (2003a) *Managing Innovation, Design, and Creativity*, London: Wiley

von Stamm, B. (2003b) *The Innovation Wave: meeting the corporate challenge*, London: Wiley

Vygotsky, L.S. (1978) *Mind in Society: the development of higher psychological processes*, Cambridge, MA: MIT Press

Wakeford, M. (2004) 'A short look at a long past', in Rabkin, N. and Redmond, R.: *Putting the Arts in the Picture: Reframing education in the 21st century*, Chicago: Columbia College

Wali, A., Severson, R. and Longoni, M. (2002) *The informal arts: finding cohesion, capacity and other cultural benefits in unexpected places*, Chicago: Chicago Center for Arts Policy, Columbia College Chicago

Walker, C. (2004) *Arts and Culture: community connections*, New York: Wallace Readers Digest Foundation

Wallinger, M. and Warnock, M. (2000) *Art for all? Their policies and our culture*, London: Peer

Watson, D. (2003) *Universities and civic engagement: a critique and a prospectus*, Key-note address of the 2nd biennial 'inside-out' conference on the civic role of universities: Charting uncertainty: capital, community and citizenship

Watson, S. and Bridge, G. (eds) (2002) *A companion to the city*, Oxford: Blackwell

Watts, J. (1981) 'Community Based Education', from Simon, B. and Taylor, W.: *Education in the Eighties; the central issues*, London: Batsford

Wells, G. (2002) 'Inquiry as an Orientation for Learning, Teaching and Teacher Education', in Wells, G. and Claxton G. *Learning for life in the 21st Century*, London: Blackwell, pp197-210

Wenger, E. (1998) *Communities of Practice: learning, meaning and identity*, Cambridge: Cambridge University Press

West, L. (2002) *Glimpses Across the Divide*, London: UEL/London Arts

White, M. (2004) 'Arts in mental health for social inclusion: towards a framework for programme evaluation', in Cowling, J. (ed) *For Art's Sake? Society and the Arts in the 21st Century*, London: Institute of Public Policy Research

Williams, R. (1959) *Culture and Society: 1780-1950*, London: Chatto and Windus

Williams, R. (1983) *Keywords: a vocabulary of culture and society*, London: Fontana

Willis, P. (1990) *Common Culture*, Buckingham: Open University Press

Willis, P. (1993) *Moving Culture,* London: Gulbenkian Foundation

Wolf, A. (2002) *Does Education Matter? Myths about education and economic growth,* London: Penguin

Woodhead, C. (2002) *Class War,* London: Little, Brown

Woolf, F. (1999) *Partnerships for learning: a guide to evaluating arts education projects,* London: Arts Council of England

Woolf, F. (2000) *From policy to partnership: developing the arts in schools,* London: Arts Council of England

Woolf, F. and Griffiths, M. (2004) *Creative Partnerships Nottingham: Action Research Phase A, setting the context,* Nottingham: Nottingham Trent University School of Education

Worpole, K. and Greenhalgh, L. (1999) *The Richness of Cities: Urban Policy in a New Landscape: Final report,* Stroud: Comedia/Demos

Young, M. (1998) *The curriculum of the future: from the new sociology of education to a critical theory of learning,* London: Falmer

Youth Music (2002) *Creating a land with music: the work, education and training of professional musicians in the 21st century,* London: Youth Music/HEFCE

Yule, W. (1998) 'The Psychological Adaptation of Refugee Children' in Rutter, J and Jones, C (eds) *Refugee Education: mapping the field,* Stoke on Trent: Trentham Books, pp79-122

Zukin, S. (1995) *The Cultures of Cities,* London: Blackwell

Zukin, S. (1989) *Loft Living: culture and capital in urban change,* Brunswick, NJ: Rutgers University Press

Subject Index

Name Index